A First Offender's Guide to Texas Criminal Courts:

Navigate the System, Protect Your Rights, Rebuild Your Life

By
Deandra M. Grant &
Douglas E. Huff

ISBN: 978-1-964281-26-1 (paperback version)
ISBN: 978-1-964281-27-8 (digital version)

MEET THE AUTHORS

DEANDRA M. GRANT, JD, GC, MS

&

DOUGLAS E. HUFF, JD

DEANDRA M. GRANT, JD, GC, MS

Deandra Grant was born in Denton but grew up in Plano and is a proud graduate of Plano Senior High School. A native Texan, her family has lived for generations in and around Gainesville, Texas.

Deandra's hard-nosed work ethic began at an early age with a variety of teenage jobs: social director at a teen nightclub, clerk at a dress shop and owner/manager of a New Orleans-style sno-cone stand (Mr Sno Ball!), to name a few.

After high school she attended Trinity University in San Antonio then came back home to Dallas for law school at SMU. Deandra has been married to Eric Clendenin for over 20 years and they have two children – Keegan and Rowan.

When not practicing law, she is very involved with dog rescue and serves as Vice President of Living the Doxie Dream Rescue & Sanctuary in Royse City. At home she and Eric have 5 rescue dachshunds and you can follow their adventures on their Instagram page @5WienerPack.

Deandra is a huge Van Halen fan (DLR – not Hagar), studies medieval European history as a hobby and loves to travel.

Lawyer Stuff:

Deandra was included in the list of Super Lawyers® for 2011-2012, 2014 – present. Super Lawyers® is an attorney rating service that is nationally recognized throughout the legal community. After performing exhaustive and rigorous research by an independent research team, they announce their list of highly capable, trustworthy, and competent attorneys in Super Lawyers® Magazine and online. The list represents no more than 5% of the attorneys in Texas.

Deandra is AV® Preeminent ™ Rated by Martindale-Hubbell®, which is the highest rating an attorney can achieve. She was given the AV® Rating for her outstanding professional achievements in the field of DWI law and her contributions to the legal community. She's also been rated 10.0 by both AVVO and Justia.

Deandra began work on The Texas DWI Manual in 2011 for James Publishing. She calls it her "labor of love". The first edition was released in 2013. It is updated annually and is considered a "must have" for attorneys defending DWI cases in Texas.

Experience:

Deandra graduated in 1990 from Trinity University in San Antonio with a B.S. in Business Administration. She earned her law degree from the SMU School of Law and was licensed by the State Bar of Texas in 1993. Having spent her last year of law school as an intern with the Dallas County District Attorney's Office, she began work there as an assistant district attorney in January 1994.

Deandra's tenure as a prosecutor focused on DWI prosecution. In 1995, she founded her own firm and began defending citizens accused of DWI and other crimes. She has practiced criminal defense for over 30 years and represents Texans charged with criminal offenses, including DWI, violent felonies, and sex crimes. As a former prosecutor, she knows firsthand how to counter the prosecutor's evidence and strategy.

Operator and Testing Experience:

Deandra has spent hundreds of hours in training courses and programs related to DWI defense. She has participated in numerous "dosing" experiments in which people are given specific amounts of alcohol over certain time periods and then tested to see the effect of the alcohol on their mental and physical capabilities. She attended and successfully completed the operator certification course for the Intoxilyzer 5000 in Florida in 2004. This was the breath-test machine used in Texas prior to the purchase of the Intoxilyzer 9000. She learned how to operate the machine and the science behind it. She has also participated in experiments related to the inaccuracy of the machine.

Deandra has completed both the student course (2008) and the instructor course (2009) on the administration of standardized field sobriety testing (SFST's), the same National Highway Traffic Safety Administration training course that teaches police officers nationwide how to identify drunk drivers during traffic stops. She now serves as an instructor of the SFST practitioner course to share the knowledge with other attorneys. In 2008, she completed coursework in Atlanta, Georgia on DWI forensic blood and urine testing.

In 2011, she began training at Axion Labs in Chicago. The courses include Forensic Chromatography, Forensic Drug Analysis and Forensic Driving Under the Influence of Drugs. She completed the coursework, passed the final exam in 2015 and was awarded the American Chemical Society Forensic Lawyer-Scientist Designation. In 2018 Deandra joined Axion Labs as an assistant chromatography instructor. She spends 5 weeks each year in Chicago at the lab.

In 2014 Deandra "went back to school". She completed a Graduate Certificate in Forensic Toxicology from the University of Florida's College of Veterinary Medicine and a Master's Degree in Pharmaceutical Science – Concentration in Forensic Science from the University of Florida's College of Pharmacy in 2016.

Deandra is a national speaker and teacher on topics including trial skills, jury selection, cross examination, field sobriety tests, drugged driving and forensic breath and blood alcohol testing. Since 2019 she's been honored to serve on the faculty of the Robert F. Borkenstein Course on the Effects of Drugs on Human Performance and Behavior.

DOUGLAS E. HUFF, JD

Attorney Douglas Huff was born in Warren, Ohio and was raised in Western Pennsylvania, outside of Pittsburgh, where he attended Mount Pleasant Area High School. After high school, Attorney Huff enlisted in the United States Army and served for four years receiving the Army Achievement Medal and the Army Commendation Medal. He received an honorable discharge after completing his full term of service and relocated to Austin, Texas.

After attending law school, Attorney Huff worked at Barbri, an organization specializing in assisting law students in studying and passing the state bar examination. In addition to being licensed to practice law in the state of Texas, he sat and passed the Oklahoma Bar during this time. Afterwards, he opened his own law practice, The Law Office of Douglas E. Huff in Dallas, Texas where he represented clients charged with various misdemeanor and felony criminal offenses.

In 2013, Attorney Huff accepted a position with the Dallas County Public Defender's Office where he worked diligently as the lead attorney in many DWI trials and other misdemeanors. Additionally, he has assisted numerous clients through plea negotiations, led many evidentiary hearings, and prepared and took part in felony trials.

Attorney Huff joined Deandra Grant Law in 2016. He became a partner in 2021. Doug is based in the Dallas office but practices throughout Texas.

On a personal note, Doug has one daughter (attorney Sorsha Huff) and a rescue dog named "Athena". He's a military vet who loves to travel. One of his favorite trips was walking the Camino de Santiago in Spain. Doug is also a competitive poker player you can often find playing in tournaments around the country.

Table of Contents

QUICK START EMERGENCY GUIDE

IF YOU'VE JUST BEEN ARRESTED - READ THIS FIRST

You're going to be okay. Thousands of people in Texas go through this every month, and the vast majority come out fine with proper guidance and legal help.

IMMEDIATE ACTIONS (First 24 Hours):

While in Jail:

- ✅ Stay calm - this is temporary
- ✅ Follow all jail rules completely
- ✅ Don't discuss your case on jail phones (they're recorded)
- ✅ Call family/friends for bail help
- ✅ Be respectful to staff and other inmates

After Release:

- ✅ Find a criminal defense attorney immediately (Chapter 3)
- ✅ Write down everything you remember about your arrest
- ✅ Follow all bond conditions exactly
- ✅ Don't contact the alleged victim if it's a domestic case

URGENT DEADLINES:

- ✅ DWI cases: Request ALR hearing within 15 days or lose license automatically
- ✅ All cases: Begin attorney search immediately
- ✅ Magistrate hearing: Usually within 48 hours of arrest

WHERE TO GET HELP RIGHT NOW:

- ✅ Mental health crisis: National Suicide Prevention Lifeline 988
- ✅ Family crisis support: 211 (dial 2-1-1 for local resources)

Remember: This guidebook will walk you through everything step by step. You don't have to figure it all out today.

YOU'RE NOT ALONE

The Reality About Criminal Charges in Texas:

Every year in Texas:

- Over 2.5 million people are arrested for various charges
- About 85% are first-time offenders like you
- Most cases (90%+) are resolved without jail time
- Thousands of people successfully rebuild their lives after criminal charges

What This Means for You:

- You're not a "criminal" - you're a person who made a mistake or got caught in circumstances
- Most people in your situation get through this and move on with their lives
- The system, while imperfect, has processes to help first-time offenders
- With proper legal help, your situation is very manageable

Success Stories Beyond Bill:

- Sarah (drug possession): Completed drug court, now works as a nurse
- Mike (DWI): Finished probation, kept his job, helps others with similar cases
- Lisa (theft): Got deferred adjudication, record sealed, promoted at work
- David (assault): Case dismissed, record expunged, went back to college

Most Important Fact: Over 75% of first-time offenders in Texas complete their cases successfully without serving jail time. You have every reason to be optimistic about your future.

FICTIONAL CHARACTER: BILL'S STORY

Meet Bill Thompson, 24, a loan officer at a regional bank in Texas. Until three months ago, Bill thought his biggest worry was making his monthly sales goals and saving for a house. His only prior contact with police was a speeding ticket, had a clean background check when he was hired at the bank, and was proud of building a solid career after college.

Everything changed on a Friday night when police arrested him after his girlfriend Sarah called 911 during a heated argument. Bill never touched Sarah, but the responding officers saw a broken lamp, redness on Sarah's arms and heard conflicting stories. Under Texas law, they arrested Bill for assault - family violence, even though Sarah immediately said she didn't want to press charges and that the lamp fell accidentally during their argument.

Now Bill faces charges that could destroy everything he's worked for. His banking career requires a clean record. His family is confused and embarrassed. Sarah wants to get back together and can't understand why "dropping charges" isn't simple. Bill is terrified, overwhelmed by legal terms he doesn't understand, and worried that even fighting the charges might cost him his job if his employer finds out about his arrest.

Throughout this guide, we'll follow Bill's journey from his arrest through the resolution of his case. You'll see how he navigates bail, finds an attorney, learns about his options like pretrial diversion, and ultimately resolves his case. Bill's story illustrates that good people can find themselves in the criminal justice system and that understanding the process is the first step toward protecting your future.

CHAPTER 1

WHAT JUST HAPPENED?

Understanding Your Arrest

If you're reading this, chances are you're feeling shocked, scared, and completely overwhelmed. Maybe you're like Bill Thompson, who just 48 hours ago was worried about nothing more serious than his monthly sales numbers at the bank where he works. Bill never imagined he'd be sitting in a jail cell, trying to process what happened when police showed up at his apartment after his girlfriend called 911 during an argument that got out of hand.

The confusion you're feeling right now is completely normal. One minute you were living your regular life, and the next minute you're being handcuffed, read your rights, and processed into the criminal justice system. Your mind is probably racing with questions: How did this happen? What comes next? Will I lose my job? What will my family think?

Take a deep breath. While being arrested is frightening and disorienting, it's important to understand that an arrest is not a conviction. You still have rights, you still have options, and you can get through this. Bill's story throughout this guide will show you that even when everything feels like it's falling apart, there's a path forward. The first step is understanding exactly what happened during your arrest and what it means for your future.

You're Not Alone in This Experience

Before we dive into the details, here's something important to know: **over 2.5 million people are arrested in Texas every year, and about 85% are first-time offenders just like you.** You're not a "criminal" – you're a person dealing with a difficult situation that thousands of others successfully navigate every month.

Your Rights During and After Arrest

Even though you're feeling overwhelmed, it's crucial to understand that being arrested doesn't strip you of your constitutional rights. When Bill Thompson heard the Miranda warning in the back of the police car, the words felt surreal – like something from a TV show rather than his real life. But those rights are real and they matter.

Miranda Rights Explained:

- **Right to remain silent:** Anything you say can and will be used against you in court. This isn't just a formality – prosecutors regularly use suspects' statements as evidence.
- **Right to an attorney:** If you can't afford one, the court will appoint one for you. Don't waive this right.
- **Understanding these rights:** Police must ensure you understand these rights before questioning you.

Bill's biggest mistake was thinking he could "explain everything" and make the charges go away. When officers asked him what happened, he tried to be helpful and cooperative. He didn't realize that his explanation of the argument with Sarah was being used to build a case against him.

The Arrest Process: What Actually Happens

The arrest process follows a predictable sequence, though it may feel chaotic when you're experiencing it:

1. **Detention and Handcuffing:** Officers will restrain you for their safety and yours
2. **Transport to Jail:** You'll be taken to the county jail or police station
3. **Booking Process:** Fingerprints, photographs, personal information, and property inventory
4. **Magistrate Warning:** Within 48 hours, you'll appear before a magistrate who will inform you of charges and set bail

What Police Can and Cannot Do

Understanding these boundaries helps you recognize if your rights were violated:

Police CAN:

- Arrest you if they have probable cause
- Search you for weapons and contraband
- Take your personal property and inventory it
- Question you after reading Miranda rights if you waive them
- Take photographs and fingerprints

Police CANNOT:

- Search your home without a warrant (with limited exceptions)
- Force you to answer questions after you invoke your right to remain silent
- Continue interrogating you after you request an attorney
- Use excessive force during arrest

Common Mistakes People Make During Arrest

Bill's attorney later identified several mistakes that made his case more difficult:

- **Talking too much:** Bill tried to explain the situation, providing statements that prosecutors later used against him
- **Consenting to searches:** When officers asked to look through his phone, Bill agreed, thinking he had nothing to hide
- **Not invoking rights clearly:** Simply staying quiet isn't enough – you must clearly state "I want to remain silent" and "I want an attorney"

Documenting Your Arrest Experience

As soon as possible after your release, write down everything you remember:

- Exact time and location of arrest
- What officers said and did
- Whether Miranda rights were read
- Any searches conducted
- Witnesses present
- Your physical and mental condition

Bill wished he had done this immediately. Weeks later, when his attorney asked for details, Bill's memory was fuzzy about crucial details that could have helped his defense.

Frequently Asked Questions

Q: Does being arrested mean I'm guilty?

A: Absolutely not. An arrest means police believe they have probable cause that you committed a crime. You're presumed innocent unless proven guilty in court.

Q: Can I be arrested if the "victim" doesn't want to press charges?

A: Yes. In Texas, the state prosecutes crimes, not individual victims. Once police make an arrest, the decision to file charges belongs to the prosecutor, not the alleged victim.

Q: What if I wasn't read my Miranda rights?

A: This doesn't automatically dismiss your case. Miranda rights only apply to custodial interrogation. If you weren't questioned, or if the questioning wasn't while you were in custody, Miranda may not apply.

Q: Should I resist if I think the arrest is unlawful?

A: Never resist arrest, even if you believe it's unlawful. Challenge the legality in court later with your attorney. Resisting can lead to additional charges and potential injury.

Remember: **Most people find the reality of the legal process less scary than their initial fears.** Like thousands of Texans before you, you can get through this successfully. Tomorrow will be easier than today as you gain knowledge and take action.

Next Steps: What Happens Now

Your arrest is just the beginning of the legal process. In the next 24-48 hours, you'll need to focus on:

- Getting released on bail
- Contacting family and friends for support
- Beginning your search for an attorney
- Avoiding any discussion of your case on jail phones

Remember Bill's experience: What felt like the end of the world was actually just the first step in a process that he successfully navigated. Your arrest doesn't define you or your future – how you handle what comes next does.

POST-ARREST CHECKLIST

Immediate Actions (First 24 Hours):

- [ ] Contact family/friends to arrange bail
- [ ] Write down everything you remember about the arrest
- [ ] Avoid discussing your case on jail phones
- [ ] Follow all jail rules and procedures
- [ ] Stay calm and cooperative with jail staff

Within 48 Hours:

- [ ] Attend magistrate warning
- [ ] Understand your bond conditions
- [ ] Begin searching for an attorney
- [ ] Gather important documents (ID, insurance, employment info)

First Week:

- [ ] Meet with potential attorneys
- [ ] Review police report when available
- [ ] Inform trusted family/friends about situation
- [ ] Begin documenting your side of events

KEY TERMS SIDEBAR

PROBABLE CAUSE

Facts and circumstances that would lead a reasonable person to believe a crime was committed and you committed it.

MIRANDA RIGHTS

Constitutional warnings police must give before custodial interrogation (questioning while you're not free to leave).

BOOKING

Administrative process of recording your arrest, taking fingerprints/photos, and inventorying personal property.

MAGISTRATE WARNING

Court appearance within 48 hours where you're formally told about charges and bail is set.

CUSTODIAL INTERROGATION

Questioning by police when you're in custody (not free to leave) and focused on obtaining incriminating statements.

BAIL/BOND

Money or conditions set by court to ensure you appear for future court dates while remaining free before trial.

⚠️

CRITICAL WARNING BOX

NEVER discuss your case on jail phones! All jail phone calls are recorded and can be used as evidence against you. Only discuss:

- ✅ Bail arrangements
- ✅ Attorney contact information
- ✅ Basic logistics (work, childcare)

Do NOT discuss:

- ❌ What happened during the incident
- ❌ Your guilt or innocence
- ❌ Details about evidence
- ❌ Witness statements

BILL'S LESSON LEARNED

"I thought being cooperative and explaining everything would help me. Instead, my statement to police became evidence against me. I should have simply said, 'I want to remain silent and I want an attorney.' Everything else could have waited until I had legal representation."

CHAPTER 2

THE FIRST 48 HOURS - Jail, Bail, and Getting Out

Right now, your priority is clear: get out of jail and start taking control of your situation. Bill Thompson learned this lesson quickly when he found himself in a Dallas County holding cell at 2 a.m., watching other inmates and wondering how long he'd be stuck there. The good news is that Bill was out on bail within 18 hours, and you can be too if you understand how the system works and take the right steps.

The first 48 hours after your arrest are critical, but they're also manageable if you know what to expect. The jail booking process, the magistrate warning, and the bail hearing are all standard procedures that happen to thousands of people every week in Texas. While it feels overwhelming and unfamiliar to you, the system is designed to process people efficiently and get them released when appropriate.

You have more control over this situation than you might think. By understanding how bail works, who to call for help, and what mistakes to avoid, you can navigate these crucial first hours and position yourself for the best possible outcome. Bill made it through this phase, and so will you. The key is staying focused, following the guidance in this chapter, and remembering that this is temporary – you will get through this and get out.

Understanding the Jail Experience

Your time in jail, however brief, will likely feel like an eternity. Bill Thompson spent 18 hours in Dallas County jail, and he later described it as one of the longest nights of his life. The key to surviving this experience is understanding that it's temporary and knowing what to expect.

The Booking Process Step-by-Step:

1. **Intake and Processing:** Personal information, medical screening, classification
2. **Property Inventory:** Your belongings are catalogued and stored
3. **Fingerprinting and Photography:** Digital prints and booking photos
4. **Medical and Mental Health Screening:** Basic health assessment
5. **Housing Assignment:** Placement in appropriate housing unit

Jail Rules and Survival Tips:

- Follow all instructions immediately and completely
- Keep to yourself and avoid discussions about your case
- Don't accept anything from other inmates
- Be respectful to staff and other inmates
- Focus on getting out, not on the injustice of being there

Bill learned quickly that arguing about his innocence or the unfairness of his situation didn't help anyone. The jail staff's job isn't to determine guilt or innocence – it's to house you safely until you can be released.

The Magistrate Warning Explained

Within 48 hours of your arrest, you must appear before a magistrate. This isn't a trial or even a hearing about your guilt or innocence. It's a procedural requirement with specific purposes:

What the Magistrate Will Do:

- Read the charges against you
- Inform you of your rights
- Set bail amount
- Impose any bond conditions

What the Magistrate Will NOT Do:

- Determine your guilt or innocence
- Dismiss your case
- Listen to your explanation of events
- Change charges based on your input

Bill expected to explain his side of the story to the magistrate and was frustrated when he realized this wasn't the purpose of the hearing. Understanding this beforehand can prevent disappointment and help you focus on what matters: getting bail set so you can be released.

Understanding Bail and Bond Options

Getting out of jail depends on making bail, and Texas offers several options:

Cash Bond:

- Pay the full bail amount in cash
- Money is returned when case concludes (minus fees)
- Most expensive upfront but cheapest long-term

Surety Bond (Bail Bondsman):

- Pay bondsman 10-20% of bail amount as a fee
- Bondsman posts full bail with court
- Fee is non-refundable even if charges are dismissed

Personal Recognizance (PR Bond):

- Released on promise to appear in court
- No money required upfront
- Typically reserved for minor charges or strong community ties

Property Bond:

- Use real estate as collateral
- Property must be worth more than bail amount
- Complex process but preserves cash

Bill's family paid a bail bondsman $2,000 (10% of his $20,000 bail) to secure his release. While this fee wasn't refundable, it allowed him to return to work and actively participate in his defense.

Bond Conditions: What You Must Follow

Most people released on bail must follow specific conditions. Violating these can result in your bond being revoked and returning to jail:

Common Bond Conditions:

- Report to pretrial services monthly
- Maintain employment or education
- Reside at specific address
- No contact with alleged victim
- No use of alcohol or drugs
- Submit to random drug testing
- Surrender passport
- No new arrests

For Domestic Violence Cases (like Bill's):

- No contact with complainant
- Stay away from complainant's home/work
- No possession of firearms
- GPS monitoring (in some cases)

Making the Most of Your Release

Once you're out on bail, your real work begins. This is your opportunity to build the strongest possible defense:

Immediate Priorities:

- Find and hire an attorney
- Gather documents and evidence
- Identify witnesses
- Begin complying with bond conditions
- Return to normal life routines

Long-term Strategy:

- Maintain steady employment
- Stay out of any trouble
- Complete any required programs early
- Document your positive activities
- Build character references

Bill used his time on bail wisely. He not only found an excellent attorney but also enrolled in anger management classes before they were required, demonstrating to the court his commitment to addressing the issues that led to his arrest.

GETTING OUT OF JAIL CHECKLIST

Before Magistrate Hearing:

- [ ] Gather emergency contact numbers
- [ ] Identify family/friends who can help with bail
- [ ] Prepare basic information (employment, residence, ties to community)
- [ ] Understand you won't be explaining your case

At Magistrate Hearing:

- [ ] Listen carefully to charges and bail amount
- [ ] Ask questions about bond conditions if unclear
- [ ] Arrange for bail payment method
- [ ] Find out when/where your next court date will be scheduled

After Release:

- [ ] Read and understand all bond conditions
- [ ] Contact family to confirm your release
- [ ] Begin attorney search immediately
- [ ] Register with pretrial services if required
- [ ] Return to work/normal routine quickly

KEY TERMS SIDEBAR

MAGISTRATE

Judicial officer who conducts initial hearings, sets bail, and ensures defendants understand their rights.

BAIL

Amount of money required to be released from jail pending trial, designed to ensure court appearances.

BOND CONDITIONS

Requirements you must follow while released on bail; violation can result in re-arrest.

PRETRIAL SERVICES

Government agency that supervises defendants released on bail and monitors compliance with bond conditions.

PERSONAL RECOGNIZANCE

Release without monetary bail based on promise to appear in court.

SURETY BOND

Bail posted by a commercial bail bondsman in exchange for a non-refundable fee.

BILL'S LESSON LEARNED

"I was so focused on explaining my innocence that I almost forgot the real goal: getting out of jail so I could fight my case properly. Once I shifted my focus to making bail and finding an attorney, everything else started falling into place. The magistrate hearing wasn't about proving I was innocent – it was about getting the process started so I could prove it later."

EMERGENCY CONTACT TEMPLATE

Information to Have Ready:

- Full legal name and date of birth
- Booking number (if known)
- Jail facility name and address
- Bail amount (after magistrate hearing)
- Bond conditions
- Next court date
- Emergency contact for bail assistance

CHAPTER 3

FINDING AND WORKING with a Criminal Defense Attorney

Let's be honest – you probably never thought you'd need a criminal defense attorney. Bill Thompson certainly didn't. When he got out of Dallas County jail on bail, his first instinct was to call his family's lawyer, the guy who helped his parents buy their house. Thankfully, that attorney was smart enough to tell Bill, "I do real estate, not criminal law. You need someone who knows what they're doing in criminal court."

Here's the thing: not all lawyers are the same, just like not all doctors are surgeons. You wouldn't want your family doctor performing heart surgery on you, and you don't want a divorce lawyer handling your criminal case. Criminal law is its own specialty, with its own rules, procedures, and strategies that can make or break your case.

I know what you're thinking – "Do I really need a lawyer? Can't I just explain what happened to the judge?" Trust me, that's not how this works. Bill thought the same thing at first. He figured he'd just tell everyone that Sarah didn't want to press charges and the whole thing would go away. What he learned is that once the state files charges, it's not up to Sarah anymore – it's up to the prosecutor. And prosecutors speak a different language than regular people.

Finding the right attorney isn't just about hiring someone with a law degree. It's about finding someone who will fight for you, explain things clearly, and guide you through a system that wasn't designed to be user-friendly.

Why Criminal Defense is Different

Criminal law isn't just another area of legal practice – it's a specialized field with its own rules, procedures, strategies, and consequences. Bill Thompson's family attorney was honest about his limitations: "I help people buy houses and write wills. Criminal defense requires knowledge I don't have and experience I haven't gained."

What Makes Criminal Defense Unique:

- **Constitutional law expertise** – Fourth, Fifth, and Sixth Amendment issues
- **Evidence rules** – What can and cannot be used against you
- **Plea negotiation skills** – Most cases resolve through bargaining, not trial
- **Trial experience** – Jury selection, cross-examination, closing arguments
- **Sentencing knowledge** – Understanding punishment ranges and alternatives
- **Local court relationships** – Knowing prosecutors, judges, and court staff

Types of Criminal Defense Attorneys

Not all criminal defense attorneys are the same. Understanding the differences helps you make the best choice for your situation:

Public Defenders:

- Court-appointed attorneys for those who cannot afford private counsel
- Experienced in criminal law but often overloaded with cases
- Free, but you must qualify based on income and the Judge can later order the repayment of legal fees at the end of your case
- Limited time for individual attention

Private Solo Practitioners:

- Individual attorneys who handle their own cases
- Often more personal attention and communication
- Fees vary widely based on experience and reputation
- May specialize in certain types of cases

Criminal Defense Firms:

- Multiple attorneys working together
- Resources for investigation, expert witnesses, support staff
- Higher fees but often more comprehensive representation
- May have attorneys who specialize in different areas

Finding Good Representation is Very Achievable

Studies show that 90% of people who hire experienced criminal defense attorneys report satisfaction with their representation and case outcomes. The key is knowing what to look for and asking the right questions – which this chapter will teach you.

What to Look for in Your Attorney

Bill interviewed three attorneys before making his decision. Here's what he learned to evaluate:

Essential Qualifications:

- Significant experience with cases similar to yours
- Active trial practice – ask about recent jury trials
- Good standing with the State Bar (check online)
- Reasonable caseload – can they give your case attention?

Red Flags to Avoid:

- Guarantees a specific outcome
- Demands full payment upfront without a written contract
- Won't explain their strategy or answer questions
- Has disciplinary actions with the State Bar
- Seems unfamiliar with local courts and prosecutors

Questions to Ask Potential Attorneys

Bill wished he had asked better questions during his initial consultations. Here are the most important ones:

About Their Experience:

- How many cases like mine have you handled?
- What were the outcomes?
- When was your last jury trial?
- Are you familiar with this court and prosecutor?

About Your Case:

- What are the strengths and weaknesses of my case?
- What's your preliminary strategy?
- What are the likely outcomes?
- How long will this process take?

About Fees and Costs:

- What is your total fee for this case?
- What does that include and exclude?
- Are there additional costs I should expect?
- Do you offer payment plans?

About Communication:

- How often will we communicate?
- Who else in your office might work on my case?
- How quickly do you return phone calls?
- Will you personally handle my court appearances?

Understanding Legal Fees

Criminal defense attorneys typically charge flat fees rather than hourly rates. This gives you predictability but requires understanding what's included:

Typical Fee Structures:

- Flat fee for entire case – Covers all work through plea
- Separate trial fee – Additional cost if case goes to trial
- Hourly billing – Less common but sometimes used for complex cases
- Payment plans – Many attorneys offer monthly payment options

What's Usually Included:

- Initial consultation and case review
- Investigation and evidence gathering
- Plea negotiations with prosecutor
- Court appearances and hearings
- Filing motions and legal research

What Often Costs Extra:

- Expert witnesses (accident reconstruction, forensics)
- Private investigators

- Appeal if convicted
- Expungement or record sealing after case ends
- Excessive court appearances due to continuances

Bill paid $9500 for his domestic violence case, which included everything through trial if necessary. His attorney was upfront that expert witnesses or a private investigator would cost additional money, but those weren't needed in his case.

Working Effectively with Your Attorney

Once you hire an attorney, your relationship becomes a partnership. Here's how to get the best results:

Your Responsibilities:

- Be completely honest about everything, even embarrassing details
- Respond promptly to requests for information or documents
- Follow all advice regarding bond conditions and court appearances
- Stay out of trouble while your case is pending
- Communicate changes in contact information, employment, or circumstances

What to Expect from Your Attorney:

- Regular communication about case developments
- Prompt responses to your questions and concerns
- Professional representation in all court proceedings
- Honest assessment of your case's strengths and weaknesses
- Strategic advice about plea offers and trial decisions

Red Flags During Representation:

- Not returning calls for days or weeks
- Appearing unprepared in court
- Pressuring you to take a plea without explanation
- Not investigating your case or gathering evidence
- Missing court dates or filing deadlines

The Attorney-Client Privilege

One of the most important protections in the legal system is attorney-client privilege. This means:

What's Protected:

- All communications between you and your attorney
- Information you provide to your attorney's staff
- Documents and evidence you share
- Strategy discussions and legal advice

What's NOT Protected:

- Communications with other people present (unless they're part of your legal team)
- Plans to commit future crimes
- Information your attorney learns from other sources

Bill was initially hesitant to tell his attorney about previous arguments with Sarah, thinking it made him look bad. His attorney explained that this information was crucial for understanding the prosecutor's likely strategy and was completely protected by privilege.

ATTORNEY SELECTION CHECKLIST

Before Initial Consultations:

☐ Research attorneys' backgrounds and experience
☐ Check State Bar records for disciplinary actions
☐ Prepare list of questions to ask
☐ Gather basic case information and documents

During Consultations:

☐ Ask about experience with similar cases
☐ Discuss fees and payment options
☐ Evaluate communication style and responsiveness
☐ Assess knowledge of local courts and prosecutors
☐ Get honest assessment of your case

Before Hiring:

☐ Review written fee agreement carefully
☐ Understand what's included and excluded
☐ Confirm availability and timeline

KEY TERMS SIDEBAR

ATTORNEY-CLIENT PRIVILEGE

Legal protection that keeps communications between you and your attorney confidential.

FLAT FEE

Single payment covering all work on your case, as opposed to hourly billing.

RETAINER

Upfront payment to secure an attorney's services, often equal to the total flat fee.

PLEA NEGOTIATION

Process of discussing potential resolutions with the prosecutor before trial.

PUBLIC DEFENDER

Court-appointed attorney for defendants who cannot afford private counsel.

CRITICAL WARNING BOX

Beware of These Red Flags:

- ⚠ Attorney guarantees specific outcome
- ⚠ Demands payment without written contract
- ⚠ Won't explain strategy or answer questions
- ⚠ Has recent disciplinary actions
- ⚠ Seems unfamiliar with your type of case

BILL'S LESSON LEARNED

"I almost hired the first attorney I called because I was panicking and wanted someone immediately. Thankfully, he was honest enough to tell me I should interview a few attorneys first. The attorney I ultimately chose wasn't the cheapest, but he had extensive experience with domestic violence cases in Dallas County and made me feel confident about my defense. That peace of mind was worth every penny."

TYPICAL FEE RANGES

Misdemeanor Cases

$3,500 - $10,000

Third Degree Felonies

$8,500 - $15,000

State Jail Felonies

$7500 - $12,000

Higher Level Felonies

$13,000+

Note:

Fees vary based on complexity, attorney experience, and local market. Always get written fee agreement.

QUESTIONS FOR INITIAL CONSULTATION

Copy and bring this list

1.

How many cases like mine have you handled?

____

____

____

____

2.

What were the typical outcomes?

____

____

____

____

3.

What are the strengths/weaknesses of my case?

____

____

____

____

4.

What's your strategy for my defense?

5.

What's your total fee and what does it include?

6.

How long will this process take?

7.

How often will we communicate?

CHAPTER 4

YOUR FIRST COURT DATE

Arraignment Explained

Your first court appearance is going to be much less dramatic than what you've seen on TV, and that's actually good news. Bill Thompson spent three sleepless nights before his arraignment, imagining worst-case scenarios and rehearsing speeches he'd never get to give. When the actual day came, he was in and out of the courtroom in less than five minutes, wondering why he'd worked himself up so much.

Here's what's really going to happen: you'll sit in a courtroom with dozens of other people, wait for your name to be called, stand up when the judge reads your charges, and then sit back down. In some counties your name won't even be called. Your attorney will speak with the district attorneys, receive a new court date from the court coordinator and then you both will leave. That's it. No dramatic speeches, no Perry Mason moments, no life-changing decisions. The arraignment is purely procedural – think of it as the court's way of officially getting your case started.

The key to handling your arraignment successfully is preparation and the right mindset. You're not there to prove your innocence or tell your side of the story. You're there to show the court that you're taking this seriously, that you understand the process, and that you're someone who deserves to remain free while your case moves forward. Bill walked into that Dallas County courtroom nervous but prepared, and he walked out with his bond intact and a clear understanding of what comes next. If there were no bond conditions added when Bill got out of jail, they were likely added at his arraignment.

By the end of this chapter, you'll know exactly what to expect, how to present yourself, and why this first court date is actually an opportunity to start your case off on the right foot.

What Really Happens at Arraignment

Arraignments are far less dramatic than most people expect. Bill Thompson spent hours mentally preparing for his first court appearance, imagining he'd have to speak publicly about his case or make important legal decisions. In reality, the entire process took less than ten minutes, and Bill barely said a word beyond "Yes, Your Honor" when asked if he could hear and understand the judge.

The Arraignment Process:

Option 1: Traditional Arraignment

- You sit in the courtroom with other defendants
- Clerk or Judge calls your name
- You stand while judge reads the charges against you
- Judge asks if you understand the charges
- Judge may add or modify bond conditions
- You receive information about your next court date

Option 2: Attorney Docket Call (More Common)

- You and your attorney appear in court

- Your attorney checks in with the court coordinator
- Attorney speaks briefly with prosecutors
- New court date is scheduled
- You may not be individually called before the judge
- Bond conditions may be discussed with court staff

Bill's arraignment followed the second format. He and his attorney arrived at 9 a.m., checked in with the court coordinator, and his attorney spent a few minutes talking with the prosecutor about the case. They received a new court date and left within 30 minutes.

Understanding Your Charges

During arraignment, you'll receive formal notice of the exact charges filed against you. This is important because it may differ from what you were initially told at arrest:

What You'll Learn:

- Specific offense you're charged with
- Degree of offense (Class A misdemeanor, third-degree felony, etc.)
- Enhancement allegations if you have prior convictions
- Date and location of alleged offense
- Case number for all future reference

Why Charges Might Change:

- Prosecutors may file additional charges after reviewing evidence
- Initial charges may be reduced based on further investigation
- Grand jury may return different charges than initially filed
- Prosecutors may add enhancement allegations for prior convictions

Bill was initially told he was arrested for "assault," but the formal charge was "Assault - Family Violence," which carries different consequences than regular assault, including potential firearm restrictions and mandatory counseling requirements.

Bond Conditions: What Gets Added

If you were released from jail without specific conditions, the arraignment is where additional restrictions are typically imposed:

Common Bond Conditions Added:

- No contact with alleged victim
- Stay away from victim's home, work, school
- Alcohol/drug restrictions and testing
- Pretrial services check-in monthly
- Maintain employment or educational enrollment
- Reside at approved address
- Surrender firearms (especially domestic violence cases)
- GPS monitoring (serious cases)

Bill's bond was initially set at $20,000 with no specific conditions. At arraignment, the judge added:

- No contact with Sarah
- No alcohol consumption
- Monthly check-ins with pretrial services
- Surrender any firearms

Court Appearance Expectations

Your behavior and appearance at arraignment sets the tone for how the court views you throughout your case:

How to Dress:

- Business attire - suit and tie for men, professional dress or suit for women
- Conservative colors - navy, black, gray, dark brown
- Clean and pressed clothing
- Minimal jewelry and accessories
- No visible tattoos if possible

How to Behave:

- Arrive 30 minutes early
- Turn off cell phone completely
- Stand when your name is called
- Address judge as "Your Honor"
- Answer only when spoken to directly
- Let your attorney do the talking
- Show respect to court staff and other defendants

Common Arraignment Mistakes

Bill observed several mistakes other defendants made that created problems:

Appearance Mistakes:

- Showing up in casual clothes or work uniforms
- Arriving late and disrupting proceedings
- Bringing small children who became disruptive
- Wearing clothing with inappropriate messages or images

Behavioral Mistakes:

- Trying to explain their case to the judge
- Arguing with prosecutors or court staff
- Talking loudly in the courtroom
- Showing disrespect or attitude toward the process
- Discussing their case with other defendants

After Arraignment: Next Steps

Arraignment is just the beginning of your court process. Here's what typically happens next:

Immediate Follow-up:

- Comply with any new bond conditions immediately

- Register with pretrial services if required
- Begin alcohol/drug testing if ordered
- Arrange for firearm surrender if required

Case Development:

- Your attorney begins discovery process
- Prosecution provides evidence to defense
- Investigation of case facts and witnesses
- Evaluation of potential defenses and motions

Timeline Expectations:

- Misdemeanor cases: 2-6 months from arraignment
- Felony cases: 6-12 months or longer
- Complex cases: May take over a year
- Quick resolutions: Possible with good plea offers

Understanding Court Scheduling

Texas courts handle thousands of cases, so understanding the scheduling process helps manage expectations:

Why Cases Get Reset:

- Attorney scheduling conflicts
- Need more time for investigation
- Plea negotiations in progress
- Court calendar overcrowded
- Witness availability issues

Types of Court Settings:

- Announcement dockets - Brief appearances to announce case status
- Pretrial conferences - Discuss case progress and potential resolution
- Motion hearings - Argue legal issues before trial
- Trial settings - Actual trial dates (often reset multiple times)

Bill's case had four court appearances over five months before resolution. Each appearance was brief, but they were necessary for his attorney to negotiate with the prosecutor and prepare his defense.

Preparing for Future Court Dates

Each court appearance is an opportunity to demonstrate your responsibility and commitment to resolving your case properly:

Ongoing Preparation:

- Always dress professionally for every court appearance
- Arrive early and check in with your attorney
- Bring required documentation (proof of counseling, employment, etc.)
- Stay informed about your case developments
- Maintain compliance with all bond conditions

ARRAIGNMENT DAY CHECKLIST

Night Before:

- [ ] Prepare professional attire
- [ ] Review bond conditions and case information
- [ ] Confirm court time and location with attorney
- [ ] Plan to arrive 15-30 minutes early
- [ ] Turn off social media notifications

Day of Arraignment:

- [ ] Dress in business attire
- [ ] Arrive 15-30 minutes early
- [ ] Follow check in instructions provided by your attorney - will vary from county to county
- [ ] Turn off cell phone completely
- [ ] Bring pen and paper for notes
- [ ] Bring identification and bond paperwork

During Court:

- [ ] Stand when your name is called
- [ ] Listen carefully to all information
- [ ] Let your attorney handle all communication
- [ ] Take notes on new bond conditions
- [ ] Get next court date information

After Arraignment:

- [ ] Review new bond conditions with attorney, if applicable
- [ ] Begin compliance immediately
- [ ] Schedule any required check-ins
- [ ] Calendar next court date
- [ ] Ask attorney about next steps

KEY TERMS SIDEBAR

ARRAIGNMENT

Court proceeding where you're formally told about charges and bond conditions may be set.

BOND CONDITIONS

Requirements you must follow while released on bail; violation can result in jail.

CASE NUMBER

Unique identifier assigned to your case for all court records and proceedings.

COURT COORDINATOR

Court staff member who manages scheduling and administrative matters.

DOCKET CALL

Court session where multiple cases are called for brief administrative matters.

ENHANCEMENT

Additional punishment exposure based on prior criminal convictions.

⚠️

CRITICAL WARNING BOX

New Bond Conditions Take Effect Immediately!

If the judge adds bond conditions at your arraignment:

- ⚠️ They are in effect as soon as court ends
- ⚠️ Violation can result in immediate arrest
- ⚠️ "I didn't understand" is not a valid excuse
- ⚠️ Ask your attorney to clarify anything confusing

Common Immediate Requirements:

- ✅ No contact orders
- ✅ Alcohol/drug testing
- ✅ Pretrial services check-in
- ✅ Firearm surrender

BILL'S LESSON LEARNED

"I was so nervous about my first court date that I couldn't sleep the night before. When I got there, I realized I had built it up in my mind to be much more dramatic than it actually was. The key was following my attorney's advice: dress professionally, arrive early, stay quiet, and let him handle everything. The judge added some bond conditions I hadn't expected, but my attorney explained them clearly afterward. It was actually a relief to finally understand what the formal charges were and what the process would look like going forward."

COURT APPEARANCE DRESS CODE

Appropriate Attire:

- ✅ Business suit or dress pants with button-down shirt
- ✅ Conservative tie for men
- ✅ Professional dress or blouse with dress pants/skirt for women
- ✅ Closed-toe dress shoes
- ✅ Minimal, conservative jewelry

Avoid:

- ❌ Jeans, shorts, or casual pants
- ❌ T-shirts, tank tops, or revealing clothing
- ❌ Sneakers, flip-flops, or casual shoes
- ❌ Hats or caps (unless religious)
- ❌ Visible tattoos or excessive jewelry

TYPICAL CASE TIMELINE AFTER ARRAIGNMENT

Weeks 1-2

Discovery begins, attorney reviews evidence

Weeks 3-8

Investigation, potential motions filed

Weeks 8-16

Plea negotiations, pretrial conferences

Weeks 16-24

Trial preparation or final plea discussions

Resolution

Case ends through plea agreement or trial

Timeline varies significantly based on county, case complexity and court schedule

CHAPTER 5

UNDERSTANDING the Charges Against You

The legal document that spells out your charges might look intimidating, but it's actually your roadmap to understanding exactly what the state has to prove against you. When Bill Thompson first saw his indictment for "Assault - Family Violence," he panicked because he didn't understand what those legal terms really meant or how they differed from what actually happened that night with Sarah.

Here's the empowering truth: those formal charges aren't just accusations – they're also limitations. The state can only convict you of exactly what's written in that document, and they have to prove every single element beyond a reasonable doubt. Think of it like a recipe: if they're missing even one ingredient, the whole case falls apart.

Understanding your charges puts you in control of your defense strategy. When Bill's attorney walked him through each element of the assault charge, Bill realized that the state had to prove he intentionally caused bodily injury to Sarah or threatened her with imminent bodily injury. Suddenly, the case became less about the general chaos of that night and more about specific legal questions: Did Bill intend to hurt Sarah? Did he threaten her? Can the state prove either of those things happened?

This chapter will teach you how to read your charging documents like a lawyer, identify the weak points in the state's case, and understand exactly what you're up against. Knowledge is power, and understanding your charges is the first step toward beating them.

Reading Your Charging Documents

The formal document that spells out your charges – whether it's called an information, indictment, or complaint – is your roadmap to understanding exactly what the state must prove to convict you. Bill Thompson's charging document looked intimidating at first glance, filled with legal language and formal accusations. But once his attorney walked him through it section by section, Bill realized it was actually a limitation on what the prosecution could do, not just an accusation against him.

Key Parts of Your Charging Document:

Header Information:

- Court and county where your case will be tried
- Case number for all future reference
- Your full legal name and any aliases
- Date the charges were filed

The Charging Language:

- Specific statute you allegedly violated
- Degree of offense (misdemeanor class or felony degree)
- Date and location of alleged offense
- Specific acts the state claims you committed

- Enhancement paragraphs for prior convictions

Elements of the Offense:

- Each element the state must prove beyond reasonable doubt
- Alternative ways the offense can be committed
- Required mental state (intentionally, knowingly, recklessly)

Bill's Information charged him with "Assault - Family Violence" under Texas Penal Code Section 22.01. The document specifically alleged that on a particular date, Bill "intentionally, knowingly, or recklessly caused bodily injury to Sarah Martinez by grabbing her arms, or alternatively, intentionally or knowingly threatened Sarah Martinez with imminent bodily injury."

Understanding Offense Classifications

Texas organizes criminal offenses into specific categories with predetermined punishment ranges:

Misdemeanors:

- Class C: Fine up to $500 (traffic tickets, minor violations)
- Class B: Up to 180 days jail, $2,000 fine
- Class A: Up to 1 year jail, $4,000 fine

Felonies:

- State Jail: 180 days to 2 years state jail, $10,000 fine
- Third Degree: 2-10 years prison, $10,000 fine
- Second Degree: 2-20 years prison, $10,000 fine
- First Degree: 5-99 years or life, $10,000 fine
- Capital: Life without parole or death penalty

Why Classification Matters:

- Determines maximum possible punishment
- Affects eligibility for probation and deferred adjudication
- Influences plea bargaining leverage
- Impacts long-term consequences (employment, licensing, etc.)

Bill's Class A misdemeanor carried a maximum of one year in county jail and a $4,000 fine, but as a first-time offender, his attorney explained that jail time was unlikely and probation was a realistic outcome.

Enhancement Allegations Explained

If you have prior criminal convictions, the state may seek enhanced punishment through enhancement paragraphs in your charging document:

Common Enhancements:

- Repeat offender: Prior misdemeanor can enhance current misdemeanor
- Habitual offender: Multiple prior felonies can dramatically increase punishment
- Deadly weapon: Use of weapon can enhance any offense
- Family violence: Prior family violence conviction enhances current family violence charge

How Enhancements Work:

- State must prove both the current offense AND the prior conviction
- Prior conviction must be properly alleged in charging document
- You can challenge the validity or existence of prior convictions
- Successful enhancement can double or triple potential punishment

Breaking Down the Elements

Every criminal offense consists of specific elements that the state must prove. Think of these as ingredients in a recipe – if the state is missing even one element, they cannot convict you:

Example: Assault (Bill's Case) The state must prove ALL of the following:

1. Identity: Bill Thompson was the person who committed the act
2. Intent: He acted intentionally, knowingly, or recklessly

3. Conduct: He caused bodily injury OR threatened imminent bodily injury
4. Result: Sarah actually suffered bodily injury OR was threatened with imminent injury
5. Family Relationship: Bill and Sarah were in a dating relationship (for family violence enhancement)

Why Elements Matter:

- State must prove EVERY element beyond reasonable doubt
- Your attorney can challenge weak elements
- Missing evidence on any element can result in dismissal
- Elements determine what evidence is relevant

Bill's attorney identified that the "bodily injury" element was problematic for the prosecution. While Sarah had redness on her arms, proving that Bill intentionally caused this injury (rather than it occurring accidentally during the argument) would be difficult.

Alternative Allegations

Many charging documents include alternative ways the same offense can be committed. This gives prosecutors flexibility but also reveals their uncertainties:

Common Alternatives:

- Different mental states: «intentionally OR knowingly OR recklessly»
- Different methods: «by striking OR by grabbing OR by pushing»
- Different results: «causing bodily injury OR threatening imminent bodily injury»

Strategic Implications:

- Prosecutors may not be sure exactly what happened
- Alternative allegations can reveal weak evidence
- Defense strategy may focus on creating doubt about all alternatives
- Jury must agree unanimously on at least one alternative

Analyzing the State's Theory

Your charging document reveals the prosecution's theory of what happened and what they think they can prove:

What to Look For:

- Specific factual allegations – what do they claim you did?
- Missing details – what facts are they NOT alleging?
- Vague language – where are they unsure about specifics?
- Inconsistencies – do the allegations make sense together?

Questions to Ask:

- Can the state prove these specific allegations?
- What evidence supports each element?
- Are there alternative explanations for the alleged facts?
- Do the allegations match the police report?

Bill noticed that his charging document alleged he "grabbed" Sarah's arms, but the police report mentioned multiple types of physical contact. This inconsistency became important for his defense strategy.

Common Charging Mistakes

Prosecutors sometimes make errors in charging documents that can benefit your defense:

Technical Errors:

- Wrong statute cited
- Incorrect degree of offense
- Missing enhancement allegations
- Defective date or location

Factual Errors:

- Allegations not supported by evidence
- Inconsistent with police reports
- Impossible timeline of events

- Wrong victim information

Legal Errors:

- Elements that don't match the statute
- Charging impossible conduct
- Missing required jurisdictional allegations

Your Role in Understanding the Charges

While your attorney will analyze the legal aspects, you play a crucial role in understanding how the charges relate to what actually happened:

What You Should Do:

- Read the charging document carefully with your attorney
- Compare allegations to your memory of events
- Identify factual inaccuracies or impossible claims
- Point out missing context that might be relevant
- Ask questions about anything you don't understand

Information to Provide Your Attorney:

- Timeline of events as you remember them
- Witness information who saw what happened
- Physical evidence that might contradict allegations
- Alternative explanations for alleged conduct
- Character evidence that contradicts the state's theory

CHARGE ANALYSIS CHECKLIST

Document Review:

- ☐ Read charging document
- ☐ Identify each element of the offense
- ☐ Note any enhancement allegations
- ☐ Check dates, locations, and victim information for accuracy

Element Analysis:

- ☐ Understand what state must prove for each element
- ☐ Identify potentially weak elements
- ☐ Consider alternative explanations for alleged facts
- ☐ Evaluate strength of identification evidence
- ☐ Assess proof of required mental state

Defense Strategy:

- ☐ Discuss factual defenses with attorney
- ☐ Consider legal challenges to charging document
- ☐ Evaluate evidence supporting each element
- ☐ Identify beneficial witnesses or evidence
- ☐ Plan investigation priorities

KEY TERMS SIDEBAR

ELEMENTS

Specific components of a crime that the state must prove beyond reasonable doubt to obtain conviction.

ENHANCEMENT

Additional punishment exposure based on prior convictions or specific circumstances.

INFORMATION/INDICTMENT

Formal charging document that specifies exactly what crimes you're accused of committing.

MENTAL STATE

Required level of intent (intentionally, knowingly, recklessly, or with criminal negligence).

ALTERNATIVE ALLEGATIONS

Different ways the same offense can be committed, giving prosecutors flexibility in proving their case.

BODILY INJURY

Physical pain, illness, or any impairment of physical condition (broader than many people think).

⚠️

CRITICAL WARNING BOX

Don't Ignore Enhancement Allegations!

If your charging document includes enhancement paragraphs:

- ⚠️ Prior convictions can dramatically increase punishment
- ⚠️ State must prove both current offense AND prior conviction
- ⚠️ You can challenge the validity of prior convictions
- ⚠️ Enhancement can turn misdemeanor into felony-level punishment

Common Enhancements in Texas:

- ✅ Repeat DWI offenses
- ✅ Habitual felony offender
- ✅ Use of deadly weapon
- ✅ Family violence repeater

BILL'S LESSON LEARNED

"When I first read my charging document, I panicked because it made everything sound so official and serious. But when my attorney broke down each element the state had to prove, I realized they had some real problems with their case. The document said I 'intentionally caused bodily injury,' but the evidence showed only minor redness that could have happened accidentally during our argument. Understanding exactly what they had to prove helped me see that the case wasn't as hopeless as I initially thought."

ELEMENT BREAKDOWN EXAMPLE

Assault - Family Violence (Bill's Case):

ELEMENT 1: IDENTITY

- State must prove Bill committed the acts
- Defense consideration: Was identification certain?

ELEMENT 2: INTENT

- State must prove intentional, knowing, or reckless conduct
- Defense consideration: Could injury have been accidental?

ELEMENT 3: CONDUCT

- State must prove he caused bodily injury OR threatened imminent bodily injury
- Defense consideration: What evidence supports this claim?

ELEMENT 4: FAMILY RELATIONSHIP

- State must prove dating relationship existed
- Defense consideration: Is this disputed or admitted?

QUESTIONS TO ASK YOUR ATTORNEY

About the Charges:

1.

What does each element mean in plain English?

2.

What evidence supports each element?

3.

Which elements might be difficult for the state to prove?

4.

Are there any errors in the charging document?

5.

Do any defenses apply to my situation?

About Enhancements:

1. Do I have any prior convictions that could enhance punishment?

2. Are the enhancement allegations accurate?

3. Can we challenge any prior convictions?

4. How much would enhancement increase my potential punishment?

CHAPTER 6

PRETRIAL DIVERSION PROGRAMS

Avoiding Conviction

Okay, here's some potentially great news: you might be able to make your charges disappear entirely without ever going to trial. I know that sounds too good to be true, but pretrial diversion programs are real, and they're designed specifically for people like you and Bill – first-time offenders who made a mistake but aren't career criminals.

Think of pretrial diversion as the criminal justice system's way of saying, "We believe you can learn from this without ruining your life." The county where he was charged offered a diversion program for first-time domestic violence offenders. Instead of rolling the dice at trial or pleading guilty, he might have a third option: complete some classes, do community service, stay out of trouble for six months, and walk away with no conviction on his record.

Now, before you get too excited, let me be real with you: not every county offers these programs, and not every charge qualifies. In most counties that have a pretrial diversion program, the district attorney must agree or recommend you for the program. Some places have great diversion options, others have limited programs, and a few counties hardly offer any at all. It's frustrating, but that's just how Texas works – what's available depends entirely on where you got arrested.

But here's why this chapter matters: if you are eligible for pretrial diversion, it's probably the best possible outcome for your case. We're talking about avoiding a conviction entirely, keeping your record clean, and moving on with your life. That's worth understanding, even if it turns out your county doesn't offer what you need.

What Are Pretrial Diversion Programs?

Pretrial diversion programs are alternatives to traditional prosecution that allow you to avoid conviction by completing specific requirements instead of going through the normal court process. Think of it as the criminal justice system's recognition that some people who get arrested aren't really criminals – they just made mistakes that can be corrected through education, community service, or treatment rather than punishment.

Diversion Programs Have Excellent Success Rates

Here's encouraging news: **of first-time offenders who complete pretrial diversion programs, 95% never face criminal charges again.** These programs work because they address underlying issues while helping you avoid the long-term consequences of conviction.

How Pretrial Diversion Works:

Application Process:

1. Attorney applies on your behalf (you cannot apply directly)
2. Prosecutor reviews your case for eligibility
3. Victim input is considered (but not controlling)
4. Program coordinator evaluates your suitability
5. Approval or denial is communicated to your attorney

Program Requirements (Typical):

- Community service hours (usually 40-120 hours)
- Educational classes (anger management, drug education, etc.)
- Restitution to victims for any damages
- Program fees (usually $300-800)
- Regular check-ins with program coordinator
- Stay out of trouble (no new arrests)

Successful Completion:

- Charges dismissed completely
- No conviction on your record
- Eligible for expungement of arrest records
- Case closed permanently

County-by-County Variations

This is where pretrial diversion gets complicated – every county in Texas makes its own rules about what programs to offer and who qualifies:

What Dallas County Offers:

- First-time DWI program
- Domestic violence diversion
- Drug possession diversion
- Shoplifting/theft diversion
- Bad check diversion

What Denton County Offers:

- Misdemeanor diversion program
- Drug possession diversion
- Theft diversion
- Bad check program

What Collin County Offers:

- First offender program

- Drug diversion
- Property crime diversion
- Case-by-case consideration

What Some Smaller Counties Offer:

- Limited or no diversion programs
- Informal prosecutor policies
- Case-by-case consideration

What Many Counties DON'T Offer:

- DWI diversion (excluded by policy)
- Violent crime diversion
- Repeat offender programs
- Programs for enhanced charges

Bill learned that if he had been arrested in a neighboring county, no diversion program would have been available for his domestic violence charge. The location of your arrest can dramatically affect your options.

Eligibility Requirements

Most pretrial diversion programs have strict eligibility criteria:

Common Requirements:

- First-time offender (no prior convictions)
- Non-violent offense (varies by program)
- Minimal criminal history (sometimes even arrests disqualify)
- Victim cooperation (not always required but helpful)
- Stable employment/housing (shows ability to complete program)
- Resident of county where charges are filed

Common Exclusions:

- DWI offenses (many counties exclude these)
- Family violence (some counties exclude, others have special programs)

- Drug delivery/sales (possession may qualify, sales typically don't)
- Cases involving weapons
- Prior deferred adjudication (even if successfully completed)

Charges That Often Qualify:

- First-time drug possession
- Shoplifting/theft under certain amounts
- Bad checks
- Minor assault cases
- Some property crimes

The Application Process

Your attorney handles the application, but you play an important role:

What Your Attorney Will Provide:

- Formal application with case details
- Character references from employers, family, community
- Employment verification and financial information
- Treatment history if applicable to your case
- Explanation of circumstances surrounding the offense

What You Need to Provide:

- Honest background information including any prior arrests
- Contact information for character references
- Employment and education history
- Explanation of what happened (through your attorney)
- Commitment to complete all program requirements

Timeline Expectations:

- Application review: 2-4 weeks
- Victim notification: 1-2 weeks
- Final decision: 1-2 weeks after victim input

- Program enrollment: Within 2 weeks of acceptance

Bill's application process took about six weeks from submission to final approval. During this time, his attorney continued preparing his defense in case diversion was denied.

Program Requirements and Expectations

Successfully completing pretrial diversion requires commitment and organization:

Community Service:

- Approved organizations only (usually nonprofit agencies)
- Documentation required (signed forms, supervisor contact)
- Quality matters (showing up and working hard)
- Completion deadlines (usually 4-6 months)

Educational Programs:

- Specific classes required (anger management, drug education, etc.)
- Certified providers only (programs must be approved)
- Attendance requirements (usually cannot miss more than 1-2 sessions)
- Completion certificates required for program file

Financial Obligations:

- Program fees (non-refundable, due at enrollment)
- Class fees (for required educational programs)
- Restitution (if victim suffered financial losses)
- Court costs (may still be required)

Behavioral Requirements:

- No new arrests (automatic program failure)
- Regular check-ins with program coordinator
- Employment/education maintenance (must remain productive)
- Compliance with any bond conditions (until program completion)

What Happens If You Don't Complete the Program

Failing to complete pretrial diversion isn't the end of the world, but it does have consequences:

Reasons for Program Failure:

- New arrest (automatic termination)
- Failure to complete requirements within time limits
- Missing too many check-ins or classes
- Non-payment of required fees
- Providing false information to program staff

Consequences of Program Failure:

- Prosecution resumes on original charges
- No credit for work already completed
- Program fees are not refunded
- Prosecutor may be less willing to negotiate pleas
- Time limits may have expired for certain defenses

Getting Back on Track:

- Some programs allow one chance to cure minor violations
- Communication is key – contact program coordinator immediately if problems arise
- Document good faith efforts to comply despite obstacles
- Attorney can sometimes negotiate program modifications

Is Pretrial Diversion Right for You?

Pretrial diversion isn't automatically the best choice for everyone:

Advantages:

- Avoid conviction entirely if successful
- Faster resolution than going to trial
- Less expensive than extended litigation
- Educational benefits from required programs

- Future expungement eligibility

Disadvantages:

- Admission of some responsibility (though not a guilty plea)
- Time and effort required to complete programs
- Financial costs of fees and programs
- Risk of prosecution if you fail to complete
- Limited availability in many counties

Questions to Consider:

- Are you willing to complete all requirements?
- Can you afford the time and money involved?
- Do you have a strong defense if the case goes to trial?
- How important is avoiding any admission of responsibility?
- What are the realistic alternatives if diversion is denied?

Bill decided pretrial diversion was worth pursuing because it offered the best possible outcome – complete dismissal of charges. Even though it required time and effort, the alternative of risking conviction at trial made diversion an easy choice.

PRETRIAL DIVERSION CHECKLIST

Before Application:

- ☐ Confirm your county offers programs for your charge type
- ☐ Verify you meet basic eligibility requirements
- ☐ Gather character references and employment information
- ☐ Understand time and financial commitments required
- ☐ Discuss pros and cons with your attorney

During Application Process:

- ☐ Provide complete, honest information to your attorney
- ☐ Respond promptly to requests for additional information
- ☐ Maintain compliance with all bond conditions
- ☐ Stay out of any new trouble
- ☐ Continue building strong character references

If Accepted:

- ☐ Enroll in program immediately upon acceptance
- ☐ Pay all required fees and costs
- ☐ Begin community service and educational requirements
- ☐ Establish regular check-in schedule
- ☐ Document all compliance efforts

Throughout Program:

- ☐ Attend all required classes and appointments
- ☐ Complete community service hours on schedule
- ☐ Maintain regular contact with program coordinator
- ☐ Keep employment/education status stable
- ☐ Avoid any new legal problems

KEY TERMS SIDEBAR

PRETRIAL DIVERSION

Alternative to prosecution allowing dismissal of charges upon completion of specific requirements.

PROGRAM COORDINATOR

Staff member who supervises diversion participants and monitors compliance.

COMMUNITY SERVICE

Unpaid work for approved nonprofit organizations as part of program requirements.

RESTITUTION

Payment to victims for financial losses caused by alleged criminal conduct.

CHARACTER REFERENCES

People who can speak positively about your reputation and likelihood of program success.

BATTERER INTERVENTION PREVENTION PROGRAM

Specialized counseling for domestic violence cases focusing on relationship dynamics and conflict resolution.

⚠️

CRITICAL WARNING BOX

Program Failure Consequences:

- ⚠️ New arrest = automatic termination
- ⚠️ Prosecution resumes on original charges
- ⚠️ Program fees are not refunded
- ⚠️ May lose negotiation leverage with prosecutor
- ⚠️ Time spent in program doesn't count toward sentence

Success Requires:

- ✅ Perfect compliance with all requirements
- ✅ No new arrests or legal problems
- ✅ Timely completion of all obligations
- ✅ Regular communication with program staff

BILL'S LESSON LEARNED

"When my attorney first mentioned pretrial diversion, I was skeptical because it seemed too good to be true. But after researching the program and understanding what was required, I realized it might be a good option to consider. The 26-week batterer intervention prevention program might help me understand relationship dynamics better, and the community service might connect me with people doing good work in the community. It would take six months of my life, but walking away with no conviction might be worth it. I only wish more counties offered these programs."

COUNTY PROGRAM AVAILABILITY

Counties with Extensive Programs:

- Dallas County
- Bexar County (San Antonio)
- Travis County (Austin)
- Tarrant County (Fort Worth)
- Denton County
- Collin County

Counties with Limited Programs:

- Most medium-sized counties
- Some rural counties
- Varies significantly by local prosecutor policies

Counties with Few/No Programs:

- Many smaller rural counties
- Counties with traditional prosecutor approaches
- Areas with limited resources

Check with local attorney about specific availability

TYPICAL PROGRAM COSTS

Program Fees:

$300-800

Educational Classes:

$200-500

Community Service:

Free

(but time intensive)

Restitution:

Varies

by victim losses

Court Costs:

May still apply

Total Cost Range

$500-1,500

Still typically less expensive than extended litigation

QUESTIONS FOR YOUR ATTORNEY

About Eligibility

1.

Does my county offer diversion for my charge?

2.

Do I meet the basic eligibility requirements?

3.

What are my chances of being accepted?

4.

How long does the application process take?

About Requirements:

1.

What specific programs would I need to complete?

2.

How long do I have to finish everything?

3.

What are the total costs involved?

4.

What happens if I have scheduling conflicts?

About Alternatives:

1. How does diversion compare to likely plea offers?

2. What are my chances at trial?

3. Should I wait to see what plea offers are available?

4. Can I apply for diversion later if plea negotiations fail?

CHAPTER 7

DEFERRED ADJUDICATION

Second Chances in Texas

I understand that facing the possibility of a conviction feels overwhelming, especially when you're trying to figure out how this will affect your future, your job, and your relationships. Bill Thompson felt the same crushing weight when his attorney first mentioned deferred adjudication. The legal terminology was confusing, and Bill was scared that any kind of plea meant giving up and accepting guilt for something he wasn't sure he was even guilty of.

It's completely natural to feel conflicted about deferred adjudication. On one hand, you want to fight the charges because you know in your heart what really happened. On the other hand, you're terrified of the consequences if you go to trial and lose. The uncertainty is exhausting, and the pressure to make the "right" decision can feel paralyzing.

Deferred adjudication exists because the legal system recognizes that good people sometimes find themselves in bad situations. It's designed for people exactly like you – individuals who aren't criminals but who got caught up in circumstances that led to criminal charges. When Bill's attorney explained that deferred adjudication could give him a path forward without a conviction, it felt like the first hopeful news he'd heard since his arrest.

This chapter will help you understand what deferred adjudication really means, not just the legal mechanics but the human impact. You'll learn how it could protect your future while acknowledging the very real commitment and risks involved. Most importantly, you'll see that accepting deferred adjudication isn't giving up – it's making a strategic decision to prioritize your long-term well-being.

What Is Deferred Adjudication?

Deferred adjudication is Texas version of a second chance. It's a special type of probation where you plead guilty or no contest to the charges, but the judge doesn't find you guilty. Instead, the judge "defers" finding you guilty and places you on community supervision (probation). If you successfully complete your probation, the judge signs a No Finding of Guilt Order and you're discharged without a conviction.

Bill Thompson's attorney explained deferred adjudication this way: "It's like the court is saying, 'We think you made a mistake, but we're not ready to call you a criminal yet. Show us you can follow the rules and make better choices, and we'll give you a clean slate.'" For Bill, this meant he could avoid having a conviction on his record while still taking responsibility for his role in the incident with Sarah.

How Deferred Adjudication Works:

The Plea Process:

1. You enter a guilty or no contest plea to the charges
2. Judge accepts your plea but doesn't find you guilty
3. Judge defers finding of guilt and places you on probation
4. Probation terms are set (length, conditions, requirements)
5. Case is continued until probation period ends

During Probation:

1. You're technically not convicted but have entered a plea
2. All probation conditions must be followed exactly
3. Regular reporting to probation officer required
4. Court retains jurisdiction over your case
5. Violation can result in conviction on original charges

Successful Completion:

1. Judge dismisses the case at end by signing a No Finding of Guilt Order
2. You're discharged without conviction
3. Case shows dismissal rather than conviction
4. May be eligible for record sealing later

Failed Completion:

1. Judge can find you guilty of original charges
2. Full punishment range is available for sentencing
3. Time on probation doesn't count toward sentence

Most People Successfully Complete Deferred Adjudication

Texas data shows that 80-85% of people successfully complete deferred adjudication, resulting in case dismissal. This high success rate reflects that most people, when given clear requirements and support, can follow through on their commitments and earn a second chance.

Deferred Adjudication vs. Regular Probation

Understanding the difference between deferred adjudication and regular probation is crucial:

Deferred Adjudication:

- No conviction if successfully completed
- Dismissal appears on record, not conviction
- More restrictive probation conditions often required

- Higher stakes if you violate probation
- Record sealing may be available later

Regular Probation:

- Conviction appears on your record immediately
- Sentence suspended but conviction remains
- Less severe violation consequences (i.e., upper ceiling on what you could be sentenced to if your probation is revoked)
- No record sealing available (conviction permanent except in limited circumstances)
- Credit for time served if probation revoked

Bill chose deferred adjudication because avoiding a conviction was crucial for his banking career. Even though it meant two years of probation instead of one year, the long-term benefits outweighed the extended supervision period.

Eligibility for Deferred Adjudication

Not everyone qualifies for deferred adjudication, and not all charges are eligible:

Who Can Get Deferred Adjudication:

- First-time offenders (usually)
- Non-violent offenders (typically)
- People with minimal criminal history
- Defendants willing to accept responsibility
- Cases where prosecution agrees to the arrangement

Charges Usually Eligible:

- Most misdemeanors (theft, assault, drug possession)
- Many non-violent felonies (fraud, property crimes)
- Drug possession cases (often encouraged)
- Some assault cases (depending on circumstances)

Charges Usually NOT Eligible:

- Serious violent felonies (murder, aggravated assault)

- Sex offenses (especially involving children)
- Offenses requiring registration (sex offender registry)
- Some repeat offenses (habitual offender cases)

Special Considerations for Certain Charges:

Even successfully completed deferred adjudication has lasting consequences for some offense types:

DWI and Domestic Violence:

- Can be used for enhancement in future similar cases
- May affect professional licensing even without conviction
- Shows up in specialized background checks

Drug Offenses:

- May affect federal student aid eligibility
- Can impact professional licenses (medical, legal, etc.)
- Shows up in employment background checks until sealed
- May affect immigration status for non-citizens

Professional License Impact:

- Many licensing boards consider deferred adjudication
- Disclosure may be required on applications
- Can affect renewals of existing licenses
- May require board review even without conviction

The Probation Experience

Deferred adjudication probation is typically more intensive than regular probation:

Common Requirements:

- Monthly reporting to probation officer
- Community service (40-200 hours typical)
- Probation fees ($60-80 per month)

- Court costs and fines (often substantial)
- No alcohol consumption (especially domestic violence cases)
- Random drug/alcohol testing as required
- Maintain employment or educational enrollment
- Complete counseling or educational programs

Special Conditions (Depending on Offense):

- Anger management classes (assault cases)
- Drug/alcohol treatment (substance-related cases)
- Theft awareness classes (property crimes)
- Restitution to victims (financial losses)
- No contact orders (domestic violence cases)

Length of Probation:

- Misdemeanors: 6 months to 2 years
- Felonies: 2 to 10 years
- Serious felonies: Up to 10 years maximum

Bill's deferred adjudication plea bargain offer included two years of probation, monthly reporting, 80 hours of community service, completion of a 26-week batterer intervention prevention program, no alcohol consumption, and no contact with Sarah. The total cost was about $3,000 including probation fees, court costs, and program expenses.

Probation Violations and Consequences

The stakes are higher with deferred adjudication because violation can result in conviction:

Types of Violations:

- New criminal charges (most serious)
- Failing drug/alcohol tests
- Missing probation appointments
- Not completing required programs
- Violating no-contact orders

- Failing to pay fees or restitution

Violation Process:

1. Motion to revoke filed by prosecutor
2. Warrant issued for your arrest (usually)
3. Hearing scheduled before original judge
4. Burden of proof is preponderance of evidence (lower than trial)
5. Judge decides whether violation occurred
6. Sentencing if violation is found

Possible Outcomes:

- Warning and continue probation
- Modify conditions (make them stricter)
- Extend probation period
- Find you guilty and sentence within full range
- Give credit for time already served on probation

Successful Completion Benefits

The rewards for successfully completing deferred adjudication are significant:

Immediate Benefits:

- No conviction on your record
- Case dismissed by the court
- Freedom from probation supervision
- Relief from probation conditions

Long-term Benefits:

- Employment applications - can honestly say «no convictions»
- Professional licensing - dismissal looks better than conviction
- Housing applications - better rental prospects
- Educational opportunities - less impact on financial aid
- Personal satisfaction - proving you can complete commitments

Future Opportunities:

- Record sealing eligibility (after waiting periods)
- Reduced background check impact
- Better plea bargaining if future charges arise
- Character evidence of rehabilitation

Making the Decision

Deciding whether to accept deferred adjudication requires careful consideration:

Factors Supporting Deferred Adjudication:

- Weak defense to the charges
- Avoiding conviction is extremely important
- Willing to comply with probation requirements
- Stable lifestyle that supports compliance
- Long-term thinking about career and future

Factors Against Deferred Adjudication:

- Strong defense that might result in dismissal or acquittal
- Unable to comply with strict probation requirements
- Financial inability to pay costs and fees
- Lifestyle incompatible with probation conditions
- Charge type that doesn't benefit from deferred adjudication

Questions to Ask Your Attorney:

- What are my chances of beating the case at trial?
- What would regular probation look like compared to deferred?
- Can this charge be sealed later if I complete deferred successfully?
- What happens to my job/license if I take deferred adjudication?
- How much will deferred adjudication cost in total?

Bill's decision came down to risk management. His attorney believed they had decent defenses, but the uncertainty of trial and the potential impact of a conviction on his banking career made deferred adjudication the safer choice.

DEFERRED ADJUDICATION DECISION CHECKLIST

Before Accepting:

- [ ] Understand all probation requirements and costs
- [ ] Confirm ability to comply with conditions for full term
- [ ] Consider impact on employment and professional licenses
- [ ] Compare to likely outcomes at trial
- [ ] Evaluate financial ability to complete successfully

If Accepting:

- [ ] Enter plea with full understanding of consequences
- [ ] Begin compliance immediately with all conditions
- [ ] Establish relationship with probation officer
- [ ] Enroll in required programs promptly
- [ ] Set up payment plan for fees and costs

During Probation:

- ☐ Report to probation officer as required
- ☐ Complete community service on schedule
- ☐ Attend all required classes and programs
- ☐ Pay all fees and restitution on time
- ☐ Avoid any new legal problems

Approaching Completion:

- ☐ Ensure all requirements are finished early
- ☐ Request early termination if eligible
- ☐ Obtain documentation of successful completion
- ☐ Plan for record sealing if eligible
- ☐ Maintain documentation for future reference

KEY TERMS SIDEBAR

DEFERRED ADJUDICATION

Special probation where judge defers finding of guilt; successful completion results in No Finding of Guilt.

COMMUNITY SUPERVISION

Texas term for probation; supervised release with conditions while case is pending completion.

MOTION TO REVOKE

Legal document filed when probation violation is alleged; can result in conviction if granted.

PREPONDERANCE OF EVIDENCE

Lower burden of proof used in probation violation hearings (more likely than not).

RECORD SEALING (NONDISCLOSURE)

Process to seal successfully completed deferred adjudication from most background checks.

ENHANCEMENT

Use of completed deferred adjudication to increase punishment in future cases (DWI, domestic violence).

⚠️

CRITICAL WARNING BOX

High Stakes of Deferred Adjudication:

- ⚠️ Violation can result in full conviction and sentencing
- ⚠️ Judge can sentence anywhere within punishment range
- ⚠️ Time on probation doesn't count toward sentence
- ⚠️ Burden of proof is lower than at trial
- ⚠️ Some charges have lasting consequences even if completed successfully

Special Warnings:

- ✅ DWI and domestic violence can be used for enhancement later
- ✅ Some charges cannot be sealed even after successful completion
- ✅ Professional licenses may be affected despite no conviction

BILL'S LESSON LEARNED

"Deciding whether to accept deferred adjudication was one of the hardest decisions I've ever made because it meant admitting I played a role in what happened that night with Sarah. But my attorney helped me understand that it wasn't about admitting guilt – it was about taking responsibility and moving forward. The two years of probation would be challenging, especially the no-alcohol requirement and monthly reporting."

DEFERRED ADJUDICATION SUCCESS RATES

Overall Completion Rate

75-85%

Misdemeanor Cases

80-90%

success rate

Felony Cases

70-80%

success rate

Common Reasons for Failure:

- New arrests (40% of failures)
- Drug/alcohol violations (25% of failures)
- Non-payment of fees (20% of failures)
- Missing appointments (15% of failures)

Success Factors:

- Stable employment
- Strong family support
- Early completion of requirements
- Regular communication with probation officer

TYPICAL DEFERRED ADJUDICATION COSTS

Court Costs

$300-500

Probation Fees

$60-80/month

Program Costs

$200-800

Community Service

free (time investment)

Restitution

Varies by case

Misdemeanor Total

$1,500-3,000

Felony Total

$3,000-6,000+

Costs vary significantly by county and case complexity

TYPICAL PROBATION LENGTHS

Class C Misdemeanor

6 months - 1 year

Class B Misdemeanor

1-2 years

Class A Misdemeanor

1-2 years

State Jail Felony

2-5 years

Third Degree Felony

2-10 years

Second Degree Felony

2-10 years

First Degree Felony

5-10 years

Length depends on charge severity and negotiations.

CHAPTER 8

PLEA BARGAINING

Negotiating Your Case

This is where you start taking control of your future. Plea bargaining isn't about giving up or admitting defeat – it's about making smart, strategic decisions that protect what matters most to you. Bill Thompson learned this when his attorney started negotiating with the Dallas County prosecutor. Instead of feeling powerless and waiting for something to happen to him, Bill became an active participant in shaping the outcome of his case.

Here's what's exciting about this phase: you have leverage. The prosecution wants to resolve cases efficiently, and your attorney knows how to use that to your advantage. Every case has strengths and weaknesses on both sides, and skilled negotiation can turn those dynamics in your favor. Bill's attorney identified problems with the state's evidence and used those issues to negotiate from a position of strength rather than desperation.

The best part? You're in the driver's seat. Your attorney will present options and recommendations, but every decision is yours to make. This is your opportunity to weigh the certainty of a negotiated outcome against the risks and potential rewards of going to trial. You get to decide what's most important – avoiding jail time, protecting your job, minimizing the impact on your record, or fighting for complete vindication.

Remember, most successful people who've been through the criminal justice system got there through smart plea bargaining, not dramatic courtroom victories. This chapter will show you how to approach negotiations strategically, ask the right questions, and make decisions that set you up for success long after your case is over. Your future is still in your hands.

Plea Bargaining Works for Most People

Over 95% of criminal cases in Texas are resolved through plea agreements, not trials. This isn't because the system is broken – it's because experienced attorneys can usually find solutions that work for everyone involved. Most defendants find acceptable resolutions that allow them to move forward with their lives.

Understanding the Plea Bargaining Process

Plea bargaining is the art of negotiation applied to criminal law. It's how most criminal cases are resolved – not through dramatic courtroom trials, but through strategic discussions between your attorney and the prosecutor about what outcome makes sense for everyone involved. Bill Thompson's case illustrates this perfectly: what started as a potential Class A misdemeanor with jail time evolved through negotiations into a manageable resolution that protected his future.

Think of plea bargaining as a business negotiation where everyone has something the other side wants. The prosecution wants to resolve cases efficiently and secure some form of accountability. You want to minimize the impact on your life and future. Your attorney's job is to find the sweet spot where both sides can live with the outcome.

How Plea Negotiations Work:

Initial Assessment:

- Prosecutor reviews evidence and determines case strength
- Defense attorney investigates and identifies weaknesses
- Both sides evaluate risks and benefits of going to trial
- Victim input is considered (but not controlling)
- Court resources and scheduling influence timing

Negotiation Process:

- Informal discussions between attorneys outside court
- Formal offers presented in writing
- Counter-offers based on case developments
- Deadlines for accepting or rejecting offers
- Final negotiations before trial date

Factors Influencing Negotiations:

- Strength of evidence against you
- Your criminal history (or lack thereof)
- Victim cooperation and impact
- Public interest in prosecution
- Court calendar pressures
- Prosecutor's policies and priorities

Types of Plea Agreements

Not all plea deals are created equal. Understanding the different types helps you evaluate what's being offered:

Charge Bargaining:

- Reduce charges to lesser offenses
- Drop some charges in multi-count cases
- Remove enhancement allegations
- Change charge type (felony to misdemeanor)

Example: Bill's assault charge could potentially be reduced to disorderly conduct

Sentence Bargaining:

- Agreed punishment within legal range
- Probation instead of jail time
- Shorter probation periods
- Reduced fines and court costs

Example: Agreeing to 1 year probation instead of risking 1 year jail

Fact Bargaining:

- Agree on version of events
- Exclude certain facts from consideration
- Stipulate to evidence to avoid embarrassing details
- Limit scope of victim impact testimony

Example: Agreeing incident was minor disagreement, not serious assault

County-by-County Negotiation Differences

Just as pretrial diversion varies by county, so do plea bargaining practices and policies:

Dallas County:

- Standard offers for first-time offenders
- Domestic violence protocol requiring specific programs
- Drug court options for possession cases
- Veteran-friendly policies for military defendants

Tarrant County:

- Conservative approach to plea bargaining
- Emphasis on accountability over leniency
- Limited deferred adjudication for some charges
- Victim input heavily weighted

Denton County:

- Flexible negotiation approach
- Case-by-case evaluation
- Good outcomes for first-time offenders
- Reasonable prosecutor attitudes

Collin County:

- Structured plea policies
- Predictable outcomes for similar cases
- Professional prosecutor approach
- Fair but firm negotiation style

Bill learned that his case's location in the county where he was charged was advantageous because they had established programs for first-time domestic violence offenders and prosecutors who were willing to consider alternatives to traditional prosecution.

Timing of Plea Negotiations

When negotiations happen can significantly affect what's offered:

Early Negotiations (First 30 Days):

- Standard offers based on charge and criminal history
- Limited case investigation by both sides
- Conservative offers (prosecutors protect themselves)
- Quick resolution possible but may not be best deal

Mid-Case Negotiations (30-90 Days):

- More investigation completed by defense
- Discovery provided by prosecution
- Better understanding of case strengths/weaknesses
- More realistic offers based on evidence

Pre-Trial Negotiations (Final 30 Days):

- All evidence known to both sides
- Motions filed and decided

- Trial preparation costs considered
- Best offers often made as trial approaches
- Last chance for negotiated resolution

Late Negotiations (Day of Trial):

- Desperation deals sometimes available
- Witness problems may surface
- Settlement pressure at maximum
- Risky strategy - may anger prosecutors

Bill's attorney advised patience, and it paid off. The initial offer was straight probation with a conviction. After three months of investigation and motion practice, the final deal was deferred adjudication.

Evaluating Plea Offers

Not every plea offer is worth accepting. Here's how to evaluate what's on the table:

Questions to Ask:

- How does this compare to likely trial outcome?
- What are total costs (financial and otherwise)?
- How does this affect my long-term goals?
- Can I comply with all requirements?
- What happens if I violate the agreement?

Factors to Consider:

- Certainty vs. uncertainty of trial outcome
- Time and expense of continued litigation
- Impact on employment and professional licenses
- Family and personal considerations

Strength of your defense case

- Red Flags in Plea Offers:
- Impossible compliance requirements
- Excessive costs you cannot afford

- Unclear terms or conditions
- Rushed decision deadlines
- No benefit over likely trial outcome

Making the Decision

The decision to accept or reject a plea offer is always yours, but it should be informed by your attorney's advice:

Your Attorney Should Explain:

- Realistic trial outcomes and their probability
- Costs and benefits of the proposed deal
- Alternative offers that might be available
- Consequences of each possible decision
- Timeline for making the decision

You Should Consider:

- Your personal priorities and goals
- Risk tolerance for uncertainty
- Ability to comply with proposed terms
- Long-term consequences of each option
- Family and financial impact

Common Decision Factors:

- Avoiding jail time at all costs
- Protecting employment or professional licenses
- Minimizing publicity or embarrassment
- Maintaining innocence vs. accepting responsibility
- Financial constraints affecting litigation

Negotiation Strategies That Work

Your attorney employs various strategies to get better plea offers:

Evidence-Based Approaches:

- Highlighting weaknesses in prosecution case
- Providing contradictory evidence or witness statements
- Filing motions to suppress evidence
- Demonstrating alternative explanations for events

Character-Based Approaches:

- Showing rehabilitation efforts already undertaken
- Providing character references from community
- Demonstrating employment and family stability
- Highlighting lack of criminal history

Practical Approaches:

- Victim cooperation or forgiveness
- Restitution offers to make victims whole
- Community service commitments
- Treatment program enrollment

Bill's attorney used multiple strategies: he highlighted inconsistencies in the police report, provided character references from Bill's employer and family, and showed that Bill had voluntarily enrolled in anger management classes before they were required.

What Happens After Accepting a Plea

Once you accept a plea agreement, the formal legal process begins:

Plea Hearing:

- Judge reviews the agreement
- You acknowledge understanding of terms
- Judge accepts or rejects the plea
- Sentence imposed or deferred as agreed
- Probation conditions explained

Important Rights You Waive:

- Right to trial by judge or jury
- Right to confront witnesses against you
- Right to remain silent (you're pleading guilty/no contest)
- Right to appeal conviction (with limited exceptions)
- Right to discovery of additional evidence

Judge's Role:

- Ensure you understand consequences of plea
- Verify plea is voluntary and not coerced
- Confirm factual basis exists for plea
- Accept or reject the agreement
- Impose sentence within agreed terms

Legal Concept: Why "The Victim Can't Drop Charges" in Criminal Cases

Simple Explanation: In Texas criminal cases, the victim doesn't "press charges" and therefore can't "drop charges." The State of Texas is the one who files criminal charges and decides whether to prosecute. Once police make an arrest and file a report, the decision to pursue criminal charges belongs entirely to the prosecutor's office, not the victim. Think of it this way: crimes are considered offenses against society as a whole, not just against individual victims.

Real-World Example: Bill Thompson's case perfectly illustrates this concept. After his arrest for domestic violence, Sarah immediately told police she didn't want Bill arrested and didn't want to "press charges." She called the prosecutor's office multiple times asking them to "drop the charges" and even wrote a letter saying the incident was blown out of proportion. Despite Sarah's wishes, the prosecutor continued with the case because:

- The State of Texas was now the "complainant," not Sarah
- Physical evidence existed (photos of Sarah's arms, the broken lamp, 911 recording)
- Texas policy treats domestic violence as a crime against

society, not just the individual

- The prosecutor's job is to enforce laws, not to follow victims' preferences

Sarah couldn't understand why her opinion didn't matter, but the prosecutor explained that allowing victims to control prosecutions would undermine the justice system and potentially put victims in danger.

Helpful Metaphor: Think of criminal charges like a traffic ticket. If a police officer sees you speeding, you get a ticket whether the other drivers on the road want you ticketed or not. The other drivers aren't the ones "pressing charges" – the State is enforcing traffic laws for everyone's safety. You can't make the ticket go away by getting other drivers to say they don't mind if you speed.

Similarly, when someone commits a crime, it's not just a problem between two people – it's society saying "this behavior violates our rules." The victim's opinion matters and is considered, but they don't get to unilaterally decide whether laws should be enforced.

Why This Matters for Defendants:

- **Don't rely on victim cooperation** as your defense strategy
- **Focus on legal defenses** and evidence rather than victim's wishes
- **Understand that victim forgiveness** doesn't equal case dismissal
- **Victim impact** is considered but doesn't control prosecution decisions
- **Plea negotiations** happen between your attorney and the prosecutor, not the victim

Why This System Exists:

- **Prevents intimidation** of victims to "drop charges"
- **Ensures consistent** law enforcement regardless of victim pressure
- **Protects society** from dangerous individuals
- **Maintains rule of law** rather than individual preferences
- **Reduces victim burden** of making prosecution decisions

This concept is especially important in domestic violence, assault, and other cases where defendants often believe victim cooperation will make their case disappear. Understanding that the State is now in control helps defendants make better strategic decisions about their defense.

PLEA EVALUATION CHECKLIST

Before Considering Offers:

- [ ] Understand all charges and potential penalties
- [ ] Review strength of prosecution evidence
- [ ] Identify potential defenses and weaknesses
- [ ] Consider personal priorities and goals
- [ ] Evaluate financial ability to continue litigation

When Evaluating Specific Offers:

- [ ] Compare offer to likely trial outcomes
- [ ] Calculate total costs of compliance
- [ ] Assess ability to meet all requirements
- [ ] Consider long-term consequences
- [ ] Discuss alternatives with attorney

Before Accepting:

- ☐ Understand all terms and conditions completely
- ☐ Confirm ability to comply with requirements
- ☐ Review waiver of rights with attorney
- ☐ Consider impact on future opportunities
- ☐ Make sure decision aligns with priorities

At Plea Hearing:

- ☐ Arrive early and professionally dressed
- ☐ Listen carefully to judge's questions
- ☐ Answer honestly about understanding terms
- ☐ Ask questions if anything is unclear
- ☐ Understand that plea is final once accepted

KEY TERMS SIDEBAR

PLEA BARGAINING

Negotiation process between prosecution and defense to resolve case without trial.

CHARGE BARGAINING

Negotiating for reduced or dismissed charges in exchange for guilty plea.

SENTENCE BARGAINING

Agreeing to specific punishment in exchange for guilty plea.

ALLOCUTION

Your statement to the court during plea hearing acknowledging facts supporting plea.

PLEA COLLOQUY

Judge's questioning during plea hearing to ensure understanding and voluntariness.

FACTUAL BASIS

Sufficient evidence to support the charges you're pleading to.

⚠️

CRITICAL WARNING BOX

Plea Agreements Are Final!

- ⚠️ Once accepted by judge, very difficult to withdraw
- ⚠️ You waive important constitutional rights
- ⚠️ Must be able to comply with all terms
- ⚠️ Violation can result in full punishment
- ⚠️ Appeals are very limited after plea

Before Accepting Any Plea:

- ✅ Fully understand all consequences
- ✅ Confirm ability to comply with terms
- ✅ Consider all alternatives thoroughly
- ✅ Make sure it aligns with your priorities

BILL'S LESSON LEARNED

"The hardest part about plea bargaining was being patient. The first offer was terrible – straight probation with a conviction that would have killed my banking career. My attorney kept telling me to wait, that better offers would come as he developed the case. He was right. After filing motions and highlighting problems with the police report, we got deferred adjudication. It took four months longer than the initial offer, but it was worth waiting for the right deal so we could discuss final options of plea vs. trial. The key was trusting my attorney's strategy and not panicking when other defendants were taking quick deals that weren't right for my situation."

TYPICAL PLEA NEGOTIATION TIMELINE

Weeks 1-4

Initial offers based on charges and criminal history

Weeks 4-12

Discovery review and case investigation

Weeks 12-20

Motion practice and evidence challenges

Weeks 20-24

Serious negotiations based on case development

Weeks 24+

Final offers as trial approaches

Timeline varies significantly by county, case complexity and court schedule

PLEA BARGAINING CONSIDERATIONS

IMMEDIATE COSTS	LONG-TERM COSTS	HIDDEN COSTS:
• Court costs and fines	• Impact on employment	• Time for compliance
• Probation fees	• Professional license effects	• Transportation for appointments
• Program costs	• Housing applications	• Lost wages for court/programs
• Restitution	• Educational opportunities	• Stress and family impact

QUESTIONS FOR YOUR ATTORNEY

About the Offer:

1. How does this compare to what I'm facing at trial?

2. What are my realistic chances of winning at trial?

3. Can we negotiate any terms of this offer?

4. What happens if I can't comply with requirements?

About Alternatives:

1.

Are there other types of pleas available?

2.

Should we wait to see if better offers come?

3.

What would happen if we file more motions?

4.

Is the prosecutor likely to get more flexible over time?

About Consequences:

1.

How will this affect my job/license/future?

2.

Can this be sealed or expunged later?

3.

What rights am I giving up by taking this plea?

4.

What exactly do I have to do to comply?

CHAPTER 9

PRETRIAL MOTIONS

and Discovery

Alright, let's talk about the part of your case that doesn't happen in front of a judge but might be the most important work your attorney does. While you're going about your daily life between court dates, your lawyer is busy playing detective, reviewing evidence, and looking for ways to poke holes in the state's case. This is where Bill Thompson's case really started to turn around, even though he barely understood what was happening at first.

Here's the thing: the prosecution doesn't just get to walk into court and say, "Trust us, this person is guilty." They have to show you their cards first. Through something called discovery, your attorney gets to see the police reports, witness statements, any videos or photos, lab results – basically everything the state plans to use against you. It's like getting to peek at your opponent's hand in a poker game.

But discovery is just the beginning. Once your attorney sees what evidence exists, they can start filing motions to challenge it. Maybe the police violated your rights during the search. Maybe the lab messed up the testing. Maybe a witness statement contradicts what's in the police report. Your attorney's job is to find these problems and ask the judge to throw out evidence that shouldn't be allowed.

Bill was amazed when his attorney found inconsistencies in the police report and problems with how the officers handled the scene. Suddenly, what seemed like a straightforward case became much more complicated for the prosecution. This chapter will help you understand what your attorney is looking for and how this behind-the-scenes work can make or break your case.

What Is Discovery and Why It Matters

Discovery is the formal process where your attorney obtains all evidence the prosecution plans to use against you. This phase is crucial because it reveals the strength of the state's case and identifies potential defense strategies.

The Michael Morton Act (named after a man wrongfully convicted and later exonerated):

- Requires prosecutors to provide all evidence related to your case upon request by the defense
- Includes evidence that might support your innocence or reduce your punishment
- Mandates disclosure of witness statements, police reports, and expert opinions
- Requires production of evidence even if prosecutors don't plan to use it at trial
- Provides penalties for prosecutors who fail to comply with discovery obligations

What discovery typically includes in criminal cases under the Michael Morton Act:

- Police reports from all responding officers

- All witness statements and interviews (not just those prosecution plans to use)
- 911 call recordings
- Photos of alleged injuries, crime scene, and defendants
- Medical records from hospitals or clinics
- Expert reports (medical, forensic, etc.)
- Video evidence from body cameras, surveillance, or cell phones
- Text messages, emails, or social media evidence
- Criminal history records
- Evidence of any weapons or physical evidence collected
- Any evidence that might support defendant's innocence or mitigate punishment

The Michael Morton Act significantly strengthened defendants' rights to discover exculpatory evidence and has helped prevent wrongful convictions in Texas criminal cases.

Bill Thompson was amazed at how much information his attorney obtained through discovery. The prosecution provided police reports, witness statements, photographs of the scene, Sarah's medical records from the hospital visit, audio recordings of the 911 call, and even text messages between Bill and Sarah from the days following the incident. Some of this evidence helped the prosecution's case, but other pieces actually supported Bill's version of events.

Types of Evidence You Can Discover:

Required Disclosure (Prosecution Must Provide):

- Police reports and supplemental reports
- Witness statements and contact information
- Physical evidence inventory and photographs
- Laboratory reports and test results
- Audio/video recordings of any kind
- Medical records related to alleged injuries
- Expert witness reports and qualifications

Optional Disclosure (You Must Request):

- Criminal histories of prosecution witnesses
- Plea agreements with cooperating witnesses
- Disciplinary records of police officers involved
- Internal affairs investigations of officers
- Evidence that was not collected or lost
- Alternative suspect information

Brady Material (Favorable Evidence):

- Evidence supporting your innocence
- Evidence undermining prosecution witnesses
- Police misconduct related to your case
- Evidence supporting your version of events

The prosecution has a constitutional duty to provide Brady material even if you don't specifically ask for it, but smart defense attorneys ask for everything anyway.

Common Types of Pretrial Motions

Pretrial motions are your attorney's tools for challenging evidence and protecting your rights before trial:

Motion to Suppress Evidence:

- Illegally seized evidence (Fourth Amendment violations)
- Statements taken without proper Miranda warnings
- Evidence from illegal searches or arrests
- Coerced confessions or statements

Motion to Dismiss:

- Insufficient evidence to support charges
- Statute of limitations has expired
- Double jeopardy violations
- Prosecutorial misconduct

Motion for Speedy Trial:

- Excessive delay in bringing case to trial
- Violation of constitutional speedy trial rights
- Prejudice caused by delay

Motion in Limine:

- Exclude prejudicial evidence that shouldn't be heard by jury
- Limit scope of witness testimony
- Prevent mention of irrelevant prior acts
- Control presentation of evidence at trial

Discovery Motions:

- Compel production of evidence prosecution is withholding
- Inspect physical evidence in person
- Interview prosecution witnesses
- Access police files and records

How Your Attorney Investigates Your Case

While the prosecution provides discovery, your attorney conducts independent investigation to build your defense:

Scene Investigation:

- Visit the location where incident occurred
- Take photographs and measurements
- Look for witnesses not contacted by police
- Check for security cameras or other recording devices
- Document conditions that might be relevant

Witness Interviews:

- Re-interview prosecution witnesses
- Find defense witnesses who support your version
- Obtain written statements from helpful witnesses
- Evaluate credibility and potential testimony
- Prepare witnesses for depositions or trial

Expert Consultation:

- Medical experts to review injury claims
- Accident reconstruction specialists
- Forensic experts to analyze physical evidence
- Character witnesses who know your reputation
- Treatment providers who can speak to rehabilitation efforts

Bill's attorney visited the apartment where the incident occurred and discovered that the neighbors who called police had a clear view into Bill's living room. When interviewed, they provided a statement that the argument appeared to be mutual and they never saw Bill strike or grab Sarah. This witness statement became crucial evidence for the defense.

Challenging Police Reports and Evidence

Police reports aren't always accurate, and your attorney's job is to find the inconsistencies and errors:

Common Police Report Problems:

- Inconsistent statements between different officers
- Timeline errors that don't match other evidence
- Missing information about witness statements
- Inaccurate descriptions of injuries or damage
- Failure to document contradictory evidence

Evidence Chain of Custody Issues:

- Improper handling of physical evidence
- Missing documentation of evidence transfers
- Contaminated samples or testing procedures
- Lost or destroyed evidence

Officer Credibility Issues:

- Disciplinary history affecting trustworthiness
- Training deficiencies in report writing or procedures
- Conflicts of interest or bias
- Past perjury or false testimony

Using Discovery to Build Your Defense

The evidence you discover often provides the foundation for your defense strategy:

Inconsistencies in the State's Case:

- Witness statements that contradict each other
- Physical evidence that doesn't support charges
- Timeline problems that make allegations impossible
- Alternative explanations for what happened

Supporting Your Version of Events:

- Evidence showing self-defense or accident
- Witness statements supporting your credibility
- Physical evidence contradicting allegations
- Character evidence showing peaceful nature

Undermining Prosecution Witnesses:

- Prior inconsistent statements
- Bias or motivation to lie
- Criminal history affecting credibility
- Substance abuse or mental health issues

Bill's case illustrates this perfectly. The initial police report made the incident sound very serious, but discovery revealed text messages where Sarah apologized to Bill and said the incident was "blown out of proportion." The 911 call audio showed Sarah was crying and upset but never claimed Bill intentionally hurt her. Medical records showed only minor bruising consistent with accidental contact during an argument.

The Motion Hearing Process

When your attorney files pretrial motions, the court holds hearings to decide them:

Before the Hearing:

- Written motions filed with legal arguments

- Evidence attached supporting the motion
- Prosecution response filed opposing the motion
- Court scheduling of hearing date

At the Hearing:

- Arguments by both sides about legal issues
- Witness testimony if facts are disputed
- Evidence presentation supporting positions
- Judge's ruling on the motion

Possible Outcomes:

- Motion granted - evidence excluded or charges dismissed
- Motion denied - evidence allowed or charges proceed
- Partial ruling - some evidence excluded, some allowed
- Deferred ruling - decision postponed until trial

Strategic Value of Motion Practice

Even motions that are denied can benefit your case:

Discovery Value:

- Learn prosecution strategy through their responses
- Identify key witnesses they plan to call
- Understand their evidence and how they'll present it
- Find weaknesses in their legal theories

Negotiation Leverage:

- Demonstrate case weaknesses to prosecutor
- Show preparedness for trial
- Create uncertainty about trial outcome
- Improve plea negotiation position

Trial Preparation:

- Preview witness testimony before trial
- Test legal theories with the judge

- Identify favorable or unfavorable judges
- Prepare for trial strategy and arguments

Bill's attorney filed three motions: to suppress Bill's statements to police (arguing they were taken without proper Miranda warnings), to exclude text messages (arguing they were taken without a warrant), and to dismiss based on insufficient evidence. Only the motion to suppress statements was granted, but all three motions revealed problems with the prosecution's case that led to better plea negotiations.

Working with Your Attorney During Investigation

Your role in the discovery and investigation process is crucial:

Information You Should Provide:

- Complete timeline of events as you remember
- Witness names and contact information
- Physical evidence location and description
- Photographs or documents you have
- Social media posts or electronic communications

Questions You Should Ask:

- What evidence supports the charges against you?
- What evidence supports your defense?
- Which witnesses are helpful or harmful?
- What motions should we file?
- How strong is the prosecution's case?

How You Can Help:

- Review discovery materials with your attorney
- Identify inaccuracies in reports or statements
- Suggest witnesses or evidence to pursue
- Provide context for evidence that seems damaging
- Be patient with the investigation timeline

Timeline Expectations

Discovery and motion practice take time, but this work is essential:

Discovery Timeline:

- Initial request: Filed within 30 days of attorney's appearance
- Prosecution response: Usually 30-60 days
- Supplemental discovery: Ongoing as new evidence develops
- Complete discovery: 3-6 months in most cases

Motion Practice Timeline:

- Motion filing: After discovery review (2-4 months)
- Prosecution response: 2-4 weeks after filing
- Hearing scheduling: 4-8 weeks later
- Court ruling: Usually immediately or within days

Investigation Timeline:

- Ongoing process: Throughout case duration
- Scene investigation: Early in case (evidence may disappear)
- Witness interviews: After discovery review
- Expert consultation: As needed based on evidence

Remember that this behind-the-scenes work often determines the outcome of your case more than what happens at trial.

DISCOVERY CHECKLIST

Information to Provide Attorney:

- [ ] Complete timeline of events as you remember
- [ ] Names and contact information for potential witnesses
- [ ] Physical evidence or documents you have access to
- [ ] Social media posts or electronic communications
- [ ] Context for evidence that seems harmful

Questions for Your Attorney:

- [ ] What is the strongest evidence against me?
- [ ] What evidence supports my defense?
- [ ] Which witnesses help or hurt my case?
- [ ] What motions should we consider filing?
- [ ] How does this discovery affect our strategy?

KEY TERMS SIDEBAR

DISCOVERY

Process of obtaining evidence from the prosecution before trial.

BRADY MATERIAL

Evidence favorable to the defense that prosecution must disclose.

MOTION TO SUPPRESS

Request to exclude illegally obtained evidence from trial.

CHAIN OF CUSTODY

Documentation showing how evidence was handled from collection to trial.

MOTION IN LIMINE

Request to exclude prejudicial evidence from being heard by jury.

PRETRIAL MOTION

Legal request filed before trial to resolve specific issues.

⚠️

CRITICAL WARNING BOX

Discovery Deadlines Matter!

- ⚠️ Your attorney must request discovery
- ⚠️ Some motions must be filed by specific deadlines
- ⚠️ Late requests may be denied by the court
- ⚠️ Prosecution continues investigating throughout case

Important Actions:

- ✅ Attorney must file discovery requests promptly
- ✅ Review all discovery materials thoroughly
- ✅ Identify motion opportunities quickly
- ✅ Maintain ongoing communication with attorney

BILL'S LESSON LEARNED

"I had no idea how much work my attorney was doing behind the scenes. While I was going about my daily life between court dates, he was reviewing police reports, interviewing witnesses, filing motions, and building my defense. The discovery process revealed text messages where Sarah apologized and said the whole thing was blown out of proportion – evidence that completely changed how the prosecutor viewed my case. I learned that patience is crucial because this investigative work takes time, but it's often what determines whether you win or lose your case. The motion hearings weren't dramatic like TV shows, but they gave my attorney leverage in plea negotiations that ultimately led to a much better outcome."

COMMON DISCOVERY MATERIALS

Always Available:

- Police reports and supplements
- Witness statements
- Physical evidence inventory
- Laboratory reports
- Audio/video recordings

Must Be Requested:

- Officer disciplinary records
- Witness criminal histories
- Expert witness information
- Evidence not collected
- Alternative suspect information

Must Be Disclosed by Prosecution:

- Brady material (favorable evidence)
- Witness plea agreements
- Evidence supporting innocence
- Police misconduct information

MOTION SUCCESS RATES

Motion to Suppress

15-25%

success rate

Motion to Dismiss

5-10%

success rate

Discovery Motions

70-80%

success rate

Motion in Limine

40-60%

success rate

Success rates vary significantly based on case facts and legal issues

Value Beyond Success:

- Negotiation leverage
- Case investigation
- Trial preparation
- Prosecutor education

TYPICAL DISCOVERY TIMELINE

Week 1-2

Attorney files discovery request

Week 4-8

Prosecution provides initial discovery

Week 8-12

Attorney reviews and investigates

Week 12-16

Supplemental discovery provided

Week 16-20

Motion practice begins

Week 20-24

Motion hearings and rulings

Timeline varies by case complexity and court schedule

CHAPTER 10

IF YOUR CASE Goes to Trial

If you decide to take your case to trial, you're exercising one of your most fundamental constitutional rights – the right to make the state prove their case beyond a reasonable doubt. This isn't a desperate last resort; it's a strategic decision that says you believe in your innocence and you're willing to trust citizens to see the truth. Bill Thompson seriously considered trial when plea negotiations stalled, and understanding the process gave him the confidence to make an informed decision about his future.

Here's what you need to know: trials are winnable, even when the evidence seems stacked against you. The prosecution might have police reports, witness statements, and physical evidence, but they still have to present a coherent story that convinces all jurors of your guilt. That's a high bar, and your attorney's job is to create reasonable doubt by highlighting inconsistencies, challenging evidence, and presenting your side of the story.

You have significant advantages at trial that many people don't realize. You don't have to prove anything – the burden is entirely on the state. You can remain silent and let your attorney do all the talking, or you can testify on your own behalf. You get to participate in selecting the jury that will decide your fate. Most importantly, you only lose if all jurors agree you're guilty – that's twelve jurors for felonies and six jurors for misdemeanors in Texas. Even one holdout juror means a mistrial and another chance.

The courtroom might feel intimidating, but remember: you belong there. This is your opportunity to fight back, to challenge the charges, and to demand that the state meet their burden of proof. Trial isn't about luck – it's about preparation, strategy, and having the courage to demand justice.

Making the Decision to Go to Trial

The decision to take your case to trial is one of the most important choices you'll make in the criminal justice process. It's not a decision to make lightly or emotionally – it should be based on a careful analysis of the evidence, your chances of success, and what you have to gain or lose. Bill Thompson seriously considered trial when plea negotiations stalled, and his attorney helped him evaluate this decision systematically rather than emotionally.

Factors Supporting Going to Trial:

- Strong defenses to the charges
- Weak prosecution evidence or unreliable witnesses
- Constitutional violations that could exclude key evidence
- Plea offers that aren't significantly better than potential trial outcomes
- Principle matters more than practical considerations
- Nothing to lose because worst-case trial outcome isn't much worse than plea offer

Factors Against Going to Trial:

- Strong prosecution case with reliable evidence
- Weak defenses that are unlikely to succeed
- Plea offers significantly better than likely trial outcome
- Cannot afford time and expense of trial
- Risk tolerance is low for uncertainty
- Collateral consequences of conviction are manageable

Bill ultimately decided against trial because his attorney negotiated a deferred adjudication plea that avoided conviction entirely. While they had some good defenses, the certainty of no conviction through the plea deal outweighed the risk of trial.

Understanding Your Right to Trial

Going to trial isn't giving up or admitting defeat – it's exercising a fundamental constitutional right:

Sixth Amendment Rights:

- Right to jury trial (or bench trial if you choose)
- Right to confront witnesses against you
- Right to compulsory process for obtaining witnesses
- Right to assistance of counsel throughout trial

Fifth Amendment Rights:

- Right to remain silent and not testify
- Protection against double jeopardy (cannot be tried twice for same offense)
- Due process protections throughout proceedings

Fourteenth Amendment Rights:

- Equal protection under the law
- Due process in state criminal proceedings

These aren't just legal technicalities – they're real protections designed to ensure fair trials and prevent wrongful convictions.

Jury Selection Process

Jury selection, called "voir dire," is actually part of your defense strategy:

How Jury Selection Works:

- Jury pool summoned from voter registration and driver's license records
- Initial questioning by judge and attorneys
- Individual questioning of potential jurors about their backgrounds and attitudes
- Challenges for cause to remove biased jurors
- Peremptory challenges to remove jurors without stating reasons
- Final jury selection of 6 (misdemeanor) or 12 (felony) jurors plus alternates

What Your Attorney Looks For:

- Fair and impartial jurors who can follow judge's instructions
- Life experiences that might make them sympathetic to your situation
- Attitudes about police and law enforcement
- Prior jury service and how they approached deliberations
- Education and employment backgrounds relevant to case issues

Red Flags in Potential Jurors:

- Strong bias toward prosecution or law enforcement
- Personal experiences similar to alleged victim
- Inability to presume innocence or require proof beyond reasonable doubt
- Unwillingness to consider your defenses
- Language barriers or comprehension problems

Trial Process Overview

Understanding what happens during trial helps you prepare mentally and strategically:

Opening Statements:

- Prosecution goes first and outlines their case
- Defense presents their theory and what evidence will show
- Not evidence but roadmap of what each side expects to prove
- Your attorney's opportunity to frame the case favorably

Prosecution Case-in-Chief:

- State presents evidence to prove each element of charges
- Witnesses testify and are cross-examined by defense
- Physical evidence introduced and explained
- Expert testimony if relevant to charges

Defense Case:

- Your choice whether to present evidence or rest
- Witnesses supporting your version of events
- Evidence contradicting prosecution claims
- Your testimony if you choose to testify

Closing Arguments:

- Both sides argue what evidence proves
- Prosecution argues guilt beyond reasonable doubt
- Defense argues reasonable doubt exists
- Final opportunity to persuade jury

Jury Deliberation:

- Jury discusses evidence in private
- Must reach unanimous verdict in criminal cases
- Can ask questions or request to see evidence again
- Returns verdict of guilty or not guilty

Your Role During Trial

While your attorney handles the legal work, your behavior and decisions matter:

Courtroom Behavior:

- Professional appearance every day (business attire)
- Calm demeanor regardless of testimony
- No reactions to witness statements or evidence
- Respectful attention to all proceedings
- Follow attorney's guidance about when to stand, sit, etc.

The Decision to Testify: This is entirely your choice, and it's one of the most important decisions you'll make:

Advantages of Testifying:

- Tell your side of the story directly to jury
- Explain circumstances that led to charges
- Show your character and demeanor to jury
- Address prosecution evidence directly
- Demonstrate honesty and willingness to be cross-examined

Disadvantages of Testifying:

- Subject to cross-examination by skilled prosecutor
- Prior statements can be used to impeach you
- Criminal history may become admissible
- Nervousness might be misinterpreted as guilt
- One mistake can undermine entire defense

Factors to Consider:

- Strength of prosecution case without your testimony
- Your ability to handle cross-examination
- Prior statements that might contradict testimony
- Criminal history that could be revealed
- Alternative ways to get your story to the jury

Understanding Reasonable Doubt

The prosecution's burden is high, but understanding exactly what it means helps you evaluate your chances:

What Reasonable Doubt Means:

- Higher than "probably guilty" or «likely guilty»
- Not beyond all possible doubt (that would be impossible)
- Doubt based on reason and common sense
- Enough doubt that reasonable person would hesitate to rely on evidence
- State must eliminate doubt based on reason

What Creates Reasonable Doubt:

- Inconsistent witness testimony
- Missing or destroyed evidence
- Alternative explanations for what happened
- Unreliable evidence or testimony
- Gaps in the timeline or logical sequence of events

What Doesn't Create Reasonable Doubt:

- Speculation without evidential support
- Sympathy for defendant's situation
- Dislike of police or prosecutors
- Mere possibility that someone else committed crime
- Defendant's failure to testify or prove innocence

Potential Trial Outcomes

Understanding all possible outcomes helps you make informed decisions:

Not Guilty Verdict:

- Complete vindication on all charges
- Immediate release from all bond conditions
- Eligible for expungement of arrest records

- No conviction or sentence
- Case permanently closed

Guilty Verdict:

- Conviction on some or all charges
- Sentencing phase follows (judge or jury decides punishment)
- Appeal rights preserved
- Sentence imposed within legal punishment range

Hung Jury (Mistrial):

- Jury cannot reach unanimous verdict
- Case can be retried by prosecution
- Negotiation opportunity may arise
- Pressure on both sides to resolve case

Partial Verdict:

- Guilty on some charges, not guilty on others
- Sentencing only on conviction charges
- Mixed outcome requiring strategic evaluation

Sentencing After Conviction

If convicted at trial, you face the sentencing process:

Who Decides Punishment:

- Your choice (made before trial) between judge or jury sentencing
- Judge sentencing typically more predictable
- Jury sentencing can be more unpredictable but sometimes more lenient
- Cannot change decision after trial begins

Sentencing Evidence:

- Punishment evidence presented by both sides
- Character witnesses can testify on your behalf
- Victim impact testimony allowed
- Prior criminal history becomes relevant

- Rehabilitation efforts can be presented

Sentencing Range:

- Judge/jury must sentence within legal range for offense
- Cannot exceed maximum punishment for charge level
- Must consider all relevant factors
- Probation eligibility depends on charge type and criminal history

Post-Trial Options

Even after conviction, you have options:

Appeal Rights:

- Automatic right to appeal conviction
- Must be filed within 30 days
- Reviews legal errors during trial
- Can result in new trial or dismissal
- Different from challenging factual findings

Motion for New Trial:

- Filed within 30 days of sentence
- Challenges trial errors or newly discovered evidence
- Rarely granted but preserves issues for appeal
- Must specify grounds for new trial

Sentence Modification:

- Limited circumstances allow sentence changes
- Early termination of probation possible
- Shock probation in some cases
- Appellate sentence review available

TRIAL DECISION CHECKLIST

Before Deciding on Trial:

- [ ] Evaluate strength of prosecution evidence objectively
- [ ] Consider quality of available defenses
- [ ] Compare plea offers to likely trial outcomes
- [ ] Assess financial and time costs of trial
- [ ] Consider impact on family and employment

If Choosing Trial:

- [ ] Understand all potential outcomes and consequences
- [ ] Prepare mentally for uncertainty and stress
- [ ] Decide on judge vs. jury sentencing before trial
- [ ] Consider whether you will testify
- [ ] Prepare for extended timeline and costs

Trial Preparation:

- [ ] Review all evidence and testimony with attorney
- [ ] Prepare for cross-examination if testifying
- [ ] Arrange time off work for trial duration
- [ ] Plan for professional appearance throughout trial
- [ ] Understand courtroom rules and procedures

KEY TERMS SIDEBAR

VOIR DIRE

Jury selection process where potential jurors are questioned about their backgrounds and attitudes.

PEREMPTORY CHALLENGE

Right to remove potential jurors without stating a reason (limited number available).

CHALLENGE FOR CAUSE

Request to remove biased juror for specific reason (unlimited if cause exists).

REASONABLE DOUBT

Standard of proof requiring state to eliminate doubt based on reason and common sense.

HUNG JURY

Jury that cannot reach unanimous verdict, resulting in mistrial.

ALLOCUTION

Defendant's opportunity to speak before sentencing.

⚠️

CRITICAL WARNING BOX

High Stakes of Trial:

- ⚠️ Sentences may be harsher after trial conviction than plea offers
- ⚠️ All evidence against you will be presented publicly
- ⚠️ Cannot control jury's decision-making process
- ⚠️ Appeal rights are limited to legal errors, not factual disputes
- ⚠️ Costs and time investment are substantial

Before Going to Trial:

- ✅ Honest assessment of evidence and defenses
- ✅ Realistic evaluation of chances for success
- ✅ Comparison to available plea agreements
- ✅ Consideration of all potential consequences

BILL'S LESSON LEARNED

"My attorney and I discussed going to trial because we had some good defenses – inconsistencies in the police report, helpful witness statements, and problems with how the investigation was conducted. When the prosecutor offered deferred adjudication, we had to make a strategic decision. Trial meant rolling the dice for complete vindication but risking conviction and a permanent record. Deferred adjudication meant taking responsibility but avoiding conviction if I completed probation successfully. It wasn't an easy choice, but looking back, the certainty of avoiding conviction was worth more to me than the chance of complete vindication. Every case is different, but for me, protecting my future was more important than proving I was right."

JURY COMPOSITION IN TEXAS

Misdemeanor Cases: 6 jurors

Felony Cases: 12 jurors

Unanimous Verdict Required: All criminal cases

Alternate Jurors: Selected in case of illness/emergency

Jury Selection Timeline:

- 1 day for simple cases
- 1-2 weeks for complex cases
- Individual questioning can be extensive in complex cases
- Both sides have challenges available

TRIAL OUTCOME STATISTICS

OVERALL CONVICTION RATE

80-85% of cases that go to trial

JURY VS. JUDGE TRIALS

Jury acquittal rates slightly higher

SENTENCE COMPARISON

Trial sentences often 20-40% higher than plea offers

APPEAL SUCCESS RATE

10-15% of criminal appeals succeed

Statistics vary significantly by charge type, jurisdiction, and case complexity

TRIAL COSTS TO CONSIDER

ATTORNEY FEES

Often additional charges for trial

EXPERT WITNESSES

$1500+ for testimony

INVESTIGATION COSTS

Private investigators, testing

LOST INCOME

Time off work for trial duration

FAMILY IMPACT

Stress and time commitment

TYPICAL ADDITIONAL COSTS:

Simple trial: $5,000-15,000
Complex trial: $15,000-50,000+
Appeal costs: $10,000-25,000

QUESTIONS FOR YOUR ATTORNEY

About Trial Strategy:

1.

What are our strongest defenses?

2.

What are the prosecution's strongest points?

3.

What are my realistic chances of acquittal?

4.

Should I testify in my own defense?

About Potential Outcomes:

1. What sentence range am I facing if convicted?

2. Should I choose judge or jury for sentencing?

3. How do likely trial outcomes compare to plea offers?

4. What are my appeal rights if convicted?

About Practical Considerations:

1.

How long will trial take?

2.

What additional costs should I expect?

3.

How will this affect my work and family?

4.

What happens if we get a hung jury?

CHAPTER 11

SENTENCING

What Happens If You're Convicted

Nobody wants to think about this chapter, but let's be real for a minute – understanding sentencing is important whether you're considering a plea deal or preparing for trial. Bill Thompson's attorney made sure he understood exactly what he was facing before making any decisions about his case. It wasn't fun to talk about, but knowing the potential consequences helped Bill make informed choices rather than decisions based on fear or wishful thinking.

Here's the deal: Texas sentencing isn't as scary or unpredictable as you might think. The legislature has set specific punishment ranges for every offense, so there are clear limits on what can happen to you. Your charge comes with a minimum and maximum sentence, and judges have to stay within those boundaries. It's not like the judge can just make up whatever punishment sounds good that day.

The good news is that for most first-time offenders, especially on non-violent charges, jail time isn't automatic. Texas judges have lots of options – probation, community service, fines, counseling programs. The system recognizes that sending people to jail is expensive and often counterproductive, so there's usually motivation to find alternatives that make more sense.

What really matters is understanding your specific situation. Bill's Class A misdemeanor assault charge carried up to a year in county jail and a $4,000 fine, but his attorney explained that as a first-time offender with a steady job, jail time was unlikely if he was convicted. That knowledge helped him evaluate his plea options realistically instead of panicking about worst-case scenarios that probably weren't going to happen.

Understanding Texas Punishment Ranges

Texas law takes the guesswork out of sentencing by establishing specific punishment ranges for each level of offense. These ranges set the boundaries within which judges and juries must operate – they can't just make up punishments that sound appropriate. Bill Thompson's Class A misdemeanor assault charge carried a punishment range of up to one year in county jail and up to a $4,000 fine, but understanding the range was just the beginning of understanding his real exposure.

Texas Offense Classifications and Punishments:

Class C Misdemeanor:

- Maximum: $500 fine only
- No jail time authorized
- Examples: Most traffic tickets, minor ordinance violations

Class B Misdemeanor:

- Jail: Up to 180 days in county jail
- Fine: Up to $2,000
- Examples: First DWI, possession of small amounts of marijuana

Class A Misdemeanor:

- Jail: Up to 1 year in county jail
- Fine: Up to $4,000
- Examples: Assault, theft $750-$2,500, second DWI

State Jail Felony:

- Confinement: 180 days to 2 years in state jail facility
- Fine: Up to $10,000
- Examples: Theft $2,500-$30,000, Drug Possession

Third Degree Felony:

- Prison: 2-10 years in Texas Department of Criminal Justice (TDCJ)
- Fine: Up to $10,000
- Examples: Evading Arrest in a Car, Theft $30,000-$150,000

Second Degree Felony:

- Prison: 2-20 years in TDCJ
- Fine: Up to $10,000
- Examples: Aggravated Assault, sexual assault

First Degree Felony:

- Prison: 5-99 years or life in TDCJ
- Fine: Up to $10,000
- Examples: Murder, Aggravated Kidnapping

Judge vs. Jury Sentencing

One of the most important strategic decisions you'll make is who will determine your punishment if you're convicted:

Choosing Judge Sentencing:

- More predictable outcomes based on judge's history
- Less emotional decision-making process
- Considers legal precedent and sentencing guidelines
- Faster process without extensive punishment hearing
- Judge sees cases like yours regularly

Choosing Jury Sentencing:

- Community perspective on appropriate punishment
- May be more sympathetic to your personal circumstances
- Less predictable but potentially more lenient
- Emotional appeal may be more effective
- Fresh perspective on your case

Key Requirements:

- Must choose in writing before trial begins
- Cannot change decision once trial starts
- Defaults to judge if no written election made
- Same jury that convicted you determines punishment
- Decision is final once made

Bill's attorney advised choosing judge sentencing if they proceeded to trial because the particular judge had a reputation for being reasonable with first-time offenders, while juries in domestic violence cases could be unpredictable.

Probation Eligibility and Types

Not everyone who gets convicted goes to jail, especially first-time offenders:

Who Can Get Probation:

- First-time offenders (generally)
- Non-violent offenses (usually)
- Stable employment and community ties
- Acceptance of responsibility for actions
- Ability to comply with supervision requirements

Types of Probation:

Regular Probation (Straight Probation):

- Conviction appears on record immediately
- Jail sentence suspended while on probation

- Violation consequences limited to original sentence range
- Credit for time served if probation is revoked

Deferred Adjudication (Pre-trial only - Not available if convicted at trial):

- No conviction if successfully completed
- Higher stakes if probation is violated
- Case dismissed upon successful completion
- May be eligible for record sealing later
- Probation Length:
- Misdemeanors: Usually 1-2 years
- Felonies: Typically 2-10 years
- Judge's discretion within statutory limits
- Early termination possible with good compliance

Institutional Sentencing Options

When jail or prison time is imposed, there are different types of facilities:

County Jail:

- Misdemeanor sentences and short felony terms
- Local facility close to home and family
- Work release programs often available
- Less restrictive than prison environment
- Maximum 2 years for any single sentence

State Jail:

- State jail felony sentences (180 days - 2 years)
- Intermediate punishment between county jail and prison
- Rehabilitation programs available
- Good time credits can reduce actual time served
- Different from regular TDCJ prison

Texas Department of Criminal Justice (Prison):

- Felony sentences over 2 years
- More restrictive environment than jail or state jail
- Further from home and family typically
- Good time and work time credits available
- Parole eligibility varies by sentence length

Factors Affecting Your Sentence

Judges and juries consider many factors when determining punishment:

Factors That Help You:

- No prior criminal history
- Stable employment and family ties
- Acceptance of responsibility for actions
- Voluntary rehabilitation efforts
- Strong character references
- Restitution paid to victims
- Community service already completed

Factors That Hurt You:

- Prior criminal convictions
- Use of weapon in offense
- Injury to victim or property damage
- Leadership role in criminal activity
- Lack of remorse or responsibility
- Violation of bond conditions during case
- Impact on victim or community

Your Criminal History's Impact:

- Enhancement allegations can increase punishment range dramatically
- Prior convictions affect probation eligibility

- Pattern of behavior shown through criminal history
- Recent convictions weigh more heavily than old ones
- Similar offenses show lack of deterrent effect

Bill's lack of any prior criminal history was his strongest asset at sentencing. His attorney also presented letters from his employer, family members, and the anger management counselor whose classes he had voluntarily attended.

The Sentencing Hearing Process

If you're convicted, the sentencing phase is your opportunity to present evidence for a lighter sentence:

Punishment Evidence:

- Character witnesses who know your reputation
- Employment records and references
- Family circumstances and support system
- Rehabilitation efforts you've undertaken
- Community ties and involvement
- Impact of incarceration on dependents

Victim Impact Evidence:

- Victim's statement about how crime affected them
- Medical expenses and lost wages
- Emotional impact on victim and family
- Request for restitution or specific punishment
- Victim's opinion on appropriate sentence

Your Right to Speak:

- Allocution - your opportunity to address the court
- Not required but often beneficial
- Show remorse and acceptance of responsibility
- Explain circumstances without making excuses
- Describe rehabilitation efforts and future plans

What NOT to Say:

- Blame others for your situation
- Make excuses or minimize your actions
- Argue about guilt (that decision is made)
- Show disrespect to victim or court
- Make promises you can't keep

Restitution and Financial Consequences

Criminal sentences often include financial obligations beyond fines:

Types of Financial Obligations:

- Restitution to victims for actual losses
- Court costs (often $300-500+)
- Probation fees ($60-80 per month)
- Program costs (classes, treatment, etc.)
- Crime victims compensation fee

Restitution Requirements:

- Compensate victims for financial losses
- Medical expenses from injuries
- Property damage or replacement costs
- Lost wages due to time off work
- Counseling costs related to the offense

Payment Plans:

- Monthly payments during probation
- Ability to pay considered by court
- Consequences for non-payment can include jail
- Civil judgment may be entered for unpaid amounts

Community Service Alternative:

- Substitute for fines in some cases
- $20 per hour credit (approximately)

- Approved organizations only
- Documentation required for credit
- Not available in all jurisdictions

Appeals and Post-Conviction Relief

Even after sentencing, you have options:

Direct Appeal:

- Automatic right for all criminal convictions
- Must be filed within 30 days of sentence
- Reviews legal errors during trial
- Can result in new trial, dismissal, or sentence reduction
- Appointed attorney available if you can't afford one

Grounds for Appeal:

- Insufficient evidence to support conviction
- Legal errors in jury instructions
- Improper admission of evidence
- Prosecutorial misconduct
- Ineffective assistance of counsel

Motion for New Trial:

- Filed within 30 days of sentence
- Newly discovered evidence
- Trial errors that affected outcome
- Rarely granted but preserves appellate issues

Other Post-Conviction Options:

- Writ of habeas corpus for constitutional violations
- Sentence modification in limited circumstances
- Early termination of probation
- Pardon from governor (extremely rare)

SENTENCING PREPARATION CHECKLIST

Before Sentencing:

- ☐ Gather character reference letters from family, employers, community
- ☐ Document any rehabilitation efforts or treatment completed
- ☐ Calculate ability to pay fines, restitution, and court costs
- ☐ Prepare statement for allocution if choosing to speak
- ☐ Arrange for family support during hearing

Character Evidence to Gather:

- ☐ Employment records and supervisor recommendations
- ☐ Educational achievements and certificates
- ☐ Community service or volunteer work documentation
- ☐ Treatment or counseling completion certificates
- ☐ Military service records if applicable

Financial Planning:

- ☐ Calculate total expected costs (fines, fees, restitution)
- ☐ Determine monthly payment ability for probation
- ☐ Arrange payment plans where possible
- ☐ Understand consequences of non-payment
- ☐ Consider community service alternatives

KEY TERMS SIDEBAR

ALLOCUTION

Defendant's opportunity to speak to the court before sentencing.

ENHANCEMENT

Use of prior convictions to increase punishment range for current offense.

RESTITUTION

Payment to victims for financial losses caused by criminal conduct.

VICTIM IMPACT STATEMENT

Testimony about how crime affected victim physically, emotionally, and financially.

GOOD TIME CREDIT

Reduction in sentence for good behavior while incarcerated.

PAROLE

Supervised early release from prison before full sentence is served.

⚠️

CRITICAL WARNING BOX

Sentencing Realities:

- ⚠️ Enhancement can dramatically increase punishment exposure
- ⚠️ Judge/jury sentencing choice must be made before trial
- ⚠️ Restitution obligations survive even bankruptcy
- ⚠️ Probation violations can result in full sentence imposition
- ⚠️ Appeal rights are limited and time-sensitive

Important Considerations:

- ✅ Understand full punishment range including enhancements
- ✅ Prepare thoroughly for sentencing hearing
- ✅ Consider long-term financial obligations
- ✅ Plan for compliance with all sentence requirements

BILL'S LESSON LEARNED

"Even though I avoided conviction through deferred adjudication, understanding the sentencing process helped me appreciate what I was facing and why negotiating was so important. My attorney explained that as a first-time offender, I would likely get probation even if convicted, but having a conviction on my record would have killed my banking career. Learning about punishment ranges and how judges make sentencing decisions helped me understand why deferred adjudication was worth the extra requirements and longer supervision period. The certainty of avoiding conviction was worth more than gambling on a lenient sentence."

FIRST OFFENDER SENTENCING TRENDS

Probation Rates for First-Time Offenders:

- Class A Misdemeanor: 85-90%
- State Jail Felony: 75-80%
- Third Degree Felony: 60-70%

Average Probation Lengths:

- Misdemeanors: 12-18 months
- State Jail Felonies: 2-3 years
- Felonies: 3-5 years

Actual sentences vary significantly based on specific facts and local practices

TYPICAL SENTENCING COSTS

Court Costs

$300-600

Probation Fees

$720-960

/year

Restitution

Varies

by victim losses

Program Costs

$200-800

Community Service

Free

but time-intensive

Total Annual Cost on Probation

$1,500-3,000+

Does not include lost wages for court appearances and programs

JUDGE VS. JURY SENTENCING COMPARISON

Judge Sentencing Advantages:

- More predictable based on history
- Less emotional decision-making
- Considers legal precedents
- Faster process

Jury Sentencing Advantages:

- Community perspective
- Potentially more sympathetic
- Less institutional bias
- Fresh eyes on case

*Success rates vary significantly by jurisdiction and case type

ENHANCEMENT IMPACT EXAMPLES

WITHOUT ENHANCEMENT

Class A Misdemeanor: Up to 1 year jail

WITH ONE PRIOR MISDEMEANOR

Enhanced to Class A: 90 days to 1 year jail (minimum required)

WITH TWO PRIOR FELONIES

Enhanced to habitual offender: 25 years to life

Enhancement consequences can be severe and should be thoroughly understood

QUESTIONS FOR YOUR ATTORNEY

About Sentencing Options:

1.

What is my realistic sentencing range if convicted?

2.

Should I choose judge or jury sentencing?

3.

What are my chances for probation vs. jail time?

4.

How do enhancements affect my punishment range?

About the Sentencing Process:

1.

What evidence should we present at sentencing?

2.

Should I speak during allocution?

3.

What character witnesses would be most helpful?

4.

How should we address the victim impact testimony?

About Post-Conviction Options:

1.

What are my appeal rights if convicted?

2.

Can sentences be modified after imposition?

3.

What are the requirements for early termination of probation?

4.

How do I preserve my appellate rights?

CHAPTER 12

LIFE AFTER COURT

Probation and Compliance

Congratulations – you've made it through the court process and avoided jail time! Whether you negotiated a plea deal or received probation after trial, you now have an incredible opportunity to put this chapter of your life behind you and move forward stronger than before. Bill Thompson felt a huge wave of relief when the judge sentenced him to two years of probation instead of jail time, but his attorney quickly reminded him that probation isn't the end of his case – it's the beginning of his comeback.

Think of probation as your chance to prove that this arrest was an exception, not a pattern. Every month you successfully complete, every requirement you fulfill on time, every clean drug test you pass is evidence that you're serious about moving forward. You're not just avoiding jail – you're actively demonstrating that you've learned from this experience and you're committed to making better choices.

Here's what's exciting: probation gives you control over your outcome. Unlike sitting in jail where time just passes, probation lets you actively work toward a better future. You can complete your community service while building new skills. You can use required counseling to actually improve your relationships. You can turn mandated classes into opportunities for personal growth. Bill decided to view his domestic violence counseling as a chance to become a better partner, not just a box to check.

The best part is that successful completion of probation often opens doors for future relief – like record sealing or early termination. Every day you stay in compliance is a day closer to putting this experience completely behind you. You've got this, and this chapter will show you exactly how to succeed.

Understanding Your Probation Requirements

Probation isn't just "staying out of trouble" – it's a detailed contract between you and the court with specific requirements that must be followed exactly. Bill Thompson learned this lesson quickly when he reported to his probation officer for the first time and received a thick packet of rules, requirements, and deadlines. What seemed like a simple agreement to "be good" was actually a comprehensive supervision program with multiple moving parts.

Standard Probation Conditions (Apply to Everyone):

- Report to probation officer as directed (usually monthly)
- Pay all fines, fees, and restitution as ordered
- Maintain steady employment or approved education program
- Reside at court-approved address
- Submit to drug/alcohol testing as required
- Complete community service hours within specified time
- Avoid contact with law enforcement (no new arrests)
- Notify probation officer of any changes in employment, residence, or circumstances

Special Conditions (Specific to Your Case):

- No alcohol consumption (common in domestic violence and DWI cases)
- Complete specialized programs (anger management, drug treatment, etc.)
- No contact with alleged victim or witnesses
- Stay away from specific locations (bars, victim's neighborhood, etc.)
- Surrender firearms and avoid weapon possession
- Submit to GPS monitoring (serious cases)
- Perform additional community service beyond standard requirements
- Attend regular counseling or therapy sessions

Bill's probation included standard conditions plus no alcohol consumption, completion of a 26-week batterer intervention prevention program, no contact with Sarah, and 80 hours of community service. Each condition had specific deadlines and compliance requirements that he had to track carefully.

Probation Success is the Norm, Not the Exception

First-time offenders have an 85% success rate completing probation without violations. This high success rate shows that with proper planning and commitment, probation is very manageable. Every day, people with cases like yours are successfully completing their probation and moving forward with their lives.

Working with Your Probation Officer

Your probation officer isn't your enemy – they're your supervisor whose job is to help you succeed while ensuring you comply with court orders:

What Probation Officers Do:

- Monitor your compliance with all court orders
- Conduct regular check-ins and progress reviews
- Verify employment, residence, and program attendance

- Administer drug/alcohol tests as required
- Write reports to the court about your progress
- Recommend modifications to probation terms when appropriate
- File violation reports when compliance problems occur

How to Build a Good Relationship:

- Be honest about challenges and problems before they become violations
- Communicate proactively about schedule changes or conflicts
- Show up on time for all appointments
- Bring required documentation (pay stubs, program certificates, community service forms)
- Ask questions when requirements are unclear
- Demonstrate genuine effort to comply with all conditions

Red Flags That Create Problems:

- Missing appointments without prior notification
- Lying about employment, residence, or program attendance
- Failing drug tests or refusing to submit to testing
- Not paying fees without discussing payment plan modifications
- Getting arrested for new charges
- Violating special conditions like no-contact orders

Bill initially struggled with the monthly reporting requirement because his work schedule conflicted with his probation officer's availability. Instead of missing appointments, he contacted his probation officer to arrange alternative meeting times. This proactive communication prevented what could have become violation reports.

Managing Probation Finances

Probation is expensive, and financial problems are one of the leading causes of probation violations:

Monthly Probation Expenses:

- Supervision fees: $60-80 per month

- Drug testing: $15-25 per test (frequency varies)
- Program costs: $50-200 per month for required classes
- Transportation: Gas, bus fare to appointments and programs
- Lost wages: Time off work for appointments and court

One-Time Expenses:

- Court costs: $300-600 (often payable over time)
- Fines: Varies by charge and sentence
- Restitution: Actual damages to victims
- Program enrollment fees: $100-500 for specialized programs

Annual Financial Impact:

- Conservative estimate: $2,000-3,000 per year
- Including lost wages: $3,000-5,000 per year
- Complex cases: $5,000+ per year

Financial Management Strategies:

- Create a probation budget early in the process
- Request payment plans for large obligations
- Prioritize payments (supervision fees usually come first)
- Communicate financial problems to probation officer before missing payments
- Consider community service alternatives where available

Staying Employed and Productive

Maintaining employment during probation is both a requirement and a necessity:

Employment Challenges:

- Time off for probation appointments and programs
- Background checks may reveal pending charges or probation status
- Professional licenses may be affected by criminal charges
- Employer policies about criminal justice involvement

- Stress and distraction affecting work performance

Strategies for Success:

- Be proactive with your employer about schedule needs
- Use vacation time or unpaid leave for appointments when possible
- Schedule appointments during lunch breaks or before/after work
- Document reliability in other areas to offset occasional absences
- Consider job changes if current employer is unsupportive

Professional License Considerations:

- Notify licensing boards as required by law
- Consult with attorney about disclosure requirements
- Document rehabilitation efforts for licensing board review
- Maintain continuing education and professional development
- Consider timing of license renewal during probation

Bill was fortunate that his bank was supportive, allowing him to adjust his schedule for probation appointments and programs. He used his lunch hour for monthly reporting and took vacation days for longer program sessions.

Successfully Completing Required Programs

Most probation sentences include mandatory programs that must be completed within specific timeframes:

Common Program Types:

- Anger management (domestic violence, assault cases)
- Substance abuse treatment (DWI, drug cases)
- Theft awareness classes (property crime cases)
- Driving safety courses (DWI, traffic cases)
- Community service supervision programs

Program Requirements:

- Enrollment within 30-60 days of probation start

- Regular attendance (usually cannot miss more than 1-2 sessions)
- Active participation and completion of assignments
- Payment of program fees (often required upfront)
- Certificate of completion provided to probation officer

Choosing Program Providers:

- Court-approved providers only (get list from probation officer)
- Location and schedule that fits your work/life schedule
- Cost comparison among approved providers
- Program reputation and completion rates
- Payment plan availability

Program Success Strategies:

- Enroll immediately after probation begins
- Attend consistently even when inconvenient
- Participate actively rather than just showing up
- Complete assignments thoughtfully and on time
- Build relationships with instructors and other participants

Bill's 26-week batterer intervention prevention program met every Tuesday evening for two hours. While it was initially inconvenient and sometimes felt repetitive, he found the program helped him understand relationship dynamics and communication skills that benefited him beyond the legal requirements.

Community Service Requirements

Community service is a common probation requirement that can be personally rewarding if approached correctly:

Typical Requirements:

- 24-200 hours depending on charge and sentence
- Completion within 4-12 months of probation start
- Approved organizations only (nonprofits, government agencies, schools)

- Supervision and documentation by organization staff
- No payment for community service work

Approved Community Service Options:

- Food banks and homeless shelters
- Animal shelters and rescue organizations
- Schools and libraries (maintenance, tutoring, events)
- Parks and recreation departments
- Hospitals and nursing homes (non-medical work)
- Community festivals and public events

Making Community Service Meaningful:

- Choose organizations that align with your interests or skills
- Develop relationships with staff and other volunteers
- Learn new skills that might benefit your career
- Document experiences for character references
- Consider continuing volunteer work after completion

Community Service Success Tips:

- Start early in your probation period
- Complete hours steadily rather than rushing at the end
- Keep detailed records of hours and activities
- Get proper documentation from supervising staff
- Maintain professional attitude and work ethic

Avoiding Probation Violations

The consequences of probation violations can be severe, so prevention is crucial:

Most Common Violations:

- New arrests (automatic violation in most cases)
- Positive drug/alcohol tests
- Missing probation appointments
- Failure to complete programs within required timeframes

- Non-payment of fees, fines, or restitution
- Violating no-contact orders
- Changing residence without permission

Early Warning Signs:

- Financial stress making payments difficult
- Employment problems affecting schedule compliance
- Relationship issues creating temptation to violate no-contact orders
- Substance abuse problems leading to failed tests
- Mental health issues affecting motivation and compliance

Prevention Strategies:

- Communicate problems early to probation officer
- Seek modifications before violations occur
- Use support systems (family, friends, counselors)
- Address underlying issues (addiction, mental health, anger)
- Stay organized with calendars and reminder systems

What Happens If You Violate

Understanding the violation process helps you respond appropriately if problems occur:

Violation Process:

1. Probation officer reports suspected violation to court
2. Motion to revoke probation filed by prosecutor
3. Warrant issued for your arrest (usually)
4. Hearing scheduled before sentencing judge
5. Burden of proof is preponderance of evidence (lower than trial)
6. Judge decides if violation occurred and appropriate response

Possible Outcomes:

- Continue probation with warning

- Modify conditions (make them stricter or add requirements)
- Extend probation period
- Impose jail time while continuing probation
- Revoke probation and impose original sentence

Violation Hearing Strategy:

- Admit responsibility for actual violations
- Explain circumstances without making excuses
- Show efforts to correct problems
- Demonstrate commitment to future compliance
- Present evidence of overall progress and success

PROBATION SUCCESS CHECKLIST

First Week of Probation:

- [ ] Meet with probation officer and understand all requirements
- [ ] Set up monthly reporting schedule that works with your job
- [ ] Enroll in all required programs immediately
- [ ] Create budget for probation-related expenses
- [ ] Organize calendar system for tracking deadlines and appointments

Monthly Maintenance:

- [ ] Report to probation officer as scheduled
- [ ] Pay all required fees and restitution
- [ ] Attend all required programs and appointments
- [ ] Complete community service hours steadily
- [ ] Document all compliance efforts

Ongoing Success Strategies:

- [ ] Communicate proactively with probation officer about any problems
- [ ] Maintain steady employment and approved residence
- [ ] Stay current on all financial obligations
- [ ] Complete programs early when possible
- [ ] Build positive relationships with program staff and probation officer

Before Probation Ends:

- [ ] Ensure all requirements are completely finished
- [ ] Obtain documentation of successful completion
- [ ] Pay any remaining balances in full
- [ ] Request early termination if eligible
- [ ] Plan for life after probation supervision

KEY TERMS SIDEBAR

PROBATION OFFICER

Court officer responsible for supervising defendants on community supervision.

MOTION TO REVOKE

Legal document filed when probation violation is alleged.

COMMUNITY SUPERVISION

Texas term for probation; supervised release with conditions.

RESTITUTION

Payment to victims for financial losses caused by criminal conduct.

PREPONDERANCE OF EVIDENCE

Lower burden of proof used in probation violation hearings.

EARLY TERMINATION

Court approval to end probation before full term is completed.

⚠️

CRITICAL WARNING BOX

Probation Violation Consequences:

- ⚠️ New arrest = almost certain violation finding
- ⚠️ Judge can impose any sentence within original range
- ⚠️ Time on probation doesn't count toward jail sentence
- ⚠️ Burden of proof is much lower than at trial
- ⚠️ No right to jury trial on violation

Success Requirements:

- ✅ Perfect compliance with ALL conditions
- ✅ Proactive communication about any problems
- ✅ Financial planning for all probation costs
- ✅ Consistent attendance at all appointments and programs

BILL'S LESSON LEARNED

"The first few months of probation were overwhelming because there were so many requirements to track – monthly reporting, program attendance, community service hours, no alcohol, no contact with Sarah, and paying fees every month. I created a detailed calendar system and set phone reminders for everything. The key was treating probation like a part-time job that required consistent attention and effort. My probation officer told me I was one of the most organized probationers she supervised, and that reputation helped when I had a work conflict and needed to reschedule an appointment. Successfully completing probation gave me confidence that I could handle complex, long-term commitments and follow through on my promises."

TYPICAL PROBATION COSTS BREAKDOWN

Monthly Expenses:

- Supervision fees: $60-80
- Drug testing: $20-40 (if required)
- Program costs: $50-150
- Transportation: $25-50

One-Time Expenses:

- Court costs: $300-600
- Program enrollment: $100-300
- Restitution: Varies by case

Annual Total

$2,000-4,000+

Does not include lost wages for appointments

PROBATION TIMELINE MANAGEWMENT

Month

1

Enroll in programs, establish routines

Months

2-6

Complete bulk of community service

Months

6-12

Finish programs, maintain compliance

Final Month

Ensure all requirements completed

Key Deadlines:

- Program enrollment: Usually within 60 days
- Community service: 4-12 months to complete
- Monthly reporting: Exact dates set by officer
- Payment schedules: Usually monthly

EMERGENCY PROBATION CONTACTS

Always Have Ready:

- Probation officer direct phone number
- After-hours probation contact
- Attorney contact information
- Program coordinator numbers
- Court clerk contact for payment questions

When to Call Immediately:

- Any arrest or police contact
- Inability to make scheduled appointment
- Job loss or major life changes
- Questions about requirement compliance

PROBATION SUCCESS FACTORS

Highest Success Rates:

- Stable employment throughout probation
- Strong family support system
- Early completion of requirements
- Proactive communication with officer
- Consistent payment of all obligations

Common Failure Factors:

- New arrests (40% of violations)
- Drug/alcohol use (25% of violations)
- Financial non-compliance (20% of violations)
- Missing appointments (15% of violations)

Success rates improve dramatically with proper planning and commitment

CHAPTER 13

CLEANING YOUR RECORD

Expungement and Record Sealing

Let's talk about something that's probably been on your mind since day one: can you ever make this whole thing go away? The short answer is maybe, but it depends on how your case was resolved and how patient you're willing to be. Bill Thompson started asking about "getting his record cleared" before his case was even over, which his attorney explained was putting the cart before the horse – but it's a completely normal question that shows you're thinking about your future.

Here's the reality: Texas does offer ways to clean up your record, but the rules are pretty specific about who qualifies and when. If your case was dismissed or you were found not guilty, you should be eligible for expungement, which completely erases the whole thing like it never happened. If you successfully completed deferred adjudication, you might qualify for record sealing (called an "order of nondisclosure"), which hides your record from most background checks but doesn't completely erase it.

The tricky part is timing. You can't just file these petitions the day after your case ends – there are waiting periods, sometimes years, depending on your charge and how your case was resolved. I know that's frustrating when you want to move on with your life immediately, but these waiting periods exist for a reason.

If Bill had been found not guilty at trial he would be able to immediately file for an expunction. But here's the thing: even when there are waiting periods, having a plan for cleaning up your record gives you something positive to work toward.

Understanding Your Record Relief Options

Texas offers two main ways to clean up your criminal record: expunction (which completely erases the record) and record sealing through an order of nondisclosure (which hides the record from most background checks). The difference between these two options is crucial, and which one applies to you depends entirely on how your case was resolved.

A person found not guilty at trial and is available to immediately file for an expunction. This means they can completely erase all traces of his arrest and charges, allowing them to legally deny the entire incident ever happened on job applications, professional licensing forms, and most other situations. But the path to record relief isn't the same for everyone – it depends on your specific case outcome and charge type.

Expunction: Complete Record Erasure

Expunction is the gold standard of record relief because it completely removes all traces of your arrest and charges:

What Gets Expunged:

- Police records of arrest and investigation

- Court records including charging documents and proceedings
- Jail booking records and photographs
- Prosecution files related to your case
- DNA samples and fingerprints collected during arrest

Who Qualifies for Expunction:

- Charges dismissed or no-billed by grand jury
- Acquittal (not guilty verdict) at trial
- Conviction reversed on appeal and charges dismissed
- Identity theft cases where you were falsely arrested
- Pardoned by governor (extremely rare)

Who Does NOT Qualify:

- Any conviction on your record (convictions cannot be expunged in Texas)
- Successful deferred adjudication (this is not a dismissal for expunction purposes)
- Probation violations that resulted in conviction
- Guilty pleas even if sentence was probated

Legal Effect of Expunction:

- Can deny arrest ever happened on applications
- No criminal record appears on background checks
- Law enforcement cannot access expunged records
- Complete legal erasure of the incident

Waiting Periods for Expunction:

Waiting periods vary depending on the level of offense and the crime charged. There are too many variations and specific rules for different crimes to list general waiting periods.

What You Need to Know:

- **Dismissals require waiting periods** based on statute of limitations for your specific charge
- **Acquittals have no waiting period** - can file immediately
- **Identity theft cases** typically have no waiting period

- **Specific crimes** may have unique waiting period requirements
- **Consult with an attorney** to determine your exact eligibility date

Exception: Some counties have local rules requiring short waiting periods even for dismissals.

Record Sealing: Hiding Your Record

If you don't qualify for expunction, record sealing through an order of nondisclosure might be available:

What Record Sealing Does:

- Hides records from most private background checks
- Prevents disclosure to private employers
- Allows you to deny conviction on most applications
- Records still exist but are sealed from public view

What Record Sealing Doesn't Do:

- Law enforcement can still see sealed records
- Government agencies may still have access
- Professional licensing boards can often still see records
- Does not completely erase records like expunction

Who Qualifies for Record Sealing:

- Successful completion of deferred adjudication
- No conviction entered in the case
- Eligible charge type (some charges cannot be sealed)
- Waiting period requirements met
- No disqualifying subsequent arrests or convictions

Charges That CANNOT Be Sealed:

- Family violence offenses (including dating violence)
- Stalking charges
- Violation of protective order
- Injury to a child, elderly, or disabled person

- Abandoning or endangering a child
- Violations involving operating a motor vehicle while intoxicated

Waiting Periods for Record Sealing:

Immediate Eligibility (No Waiting Period):

- Class C misdemeanors (traffic tickets, minor offenses)

Two-Year Waiting Period:

- Class B and A misdemeanors (after completing deferred adjudication)

Five-Year Waiting Period:

- Most felonies (after completing deferred adjudication)
- Some specific misdemeanors by statute

Never Eligible:

- Sexual offenses involving children
- Human trafficking
- Family violence (including dating violence)

The Petition Process

Both expunction and record sealing require filing a petition with the court:

Steps in the Process:

1. Determine eligibility and gather required documentation
2. File petition with appropriate court (usually where case was handled)
3. Serve notice on law enforcement agencies and prosecutor
4. Wait for responses (agencies can object to petition)
5. Attend hearing if required by court or if objections filed
6. Receive court order granting or denying petition

Required Documentation:

- Certified copies of court records showing case disposition
- Criminal history background check showing your record

- Fingerprint cards for some types of petitions
- Sworn affidavit detailing grounds for relief
- Service documentation proving notice to required agencies

Timeline Expectations:

- Uncontested cases: 2-6 months from filing
- Contested cases: 4-8 months or longer
- Complex cases: May take over a year

Costs and Fees:

- Court filing fees: $300-500
- Service fees: $100-200
- Attorney fees: $1,500-3,500
- Background check fees: $25-50
- Certified copy fees: $1-5 per document

Do You Need an Attorney?

Yes. These are very detail-oriented filings and your Petition can be denied if you do not follow all the requirements set out in the law.

Benefits of Attorney Representation:

- Proper preparation of all required documents
- Knowledge of local court procedures and preferences
- Ability to argue contested cases effectively
- Experience with objections from law enforcement
- Higher success rates than pro se petitions

Red Flags Requiring Attorney:

- Law enforcement objections to your petition
- Complex case history with multiple charges
- Uncertainty about eligibility requirements
- Professional license implications
- Prior failed attempts at record relief

Special Considerations for Different Charge Types

Some offenses have unique rules and limitations:

DWI Cases:

- Cannot be expunged if there was a conviction
- Deferred adjudication allows record sealing after 2-5 years
- Sealed DWI can still be used for enhancement in future DWI cases
- Professional licenses may still be affected

Family Violence Cases:

- Cannot be sealed even with successful deferred adjudication
- Expunction available only if charges dismissed or acquittal
- Enhanced penalties for future family violence regardless of record relief
- Federal firearm restrictions may still apply

Drug Cases:

- Standard expunction/sealing rules apply
- Professional licensing may still be affected
- Federal student aid eligibility may be restored after sealing
- Immigration consequences may persist despite record relief

Maintaining Your Clean Record

Once you obtain record relief, protecting that clean record is crucial:

After Expunction:

- Legally deny the arrest ever happened
- Update all applications and forms accordingly
- Keep expunction order for your records
- Monitor background checks to ensure compliance

After Record Sealing:

- Most applications can be answered as «no conviction»

- Law enforcement contacts may still reveal sealed records
- Professional licensing may require disclosure despite sealing
- Keep nondisclosure order for reference

Ongoing Monitoring:

- Annual background checks on yourself to verify compliance
- Correct any errors that appear despite court orders
- Update employment records that may still show old information
- Maintain documentation of record relief for future reference

Future Legal Problems:

- New arrests don't affect existing expunctions
- Sealed records may become relevant in new cases
- Professional licensing issues may arise despite record relief

RECORD RELIEF ELIGIBILITY CHECKLIST

Expunction Eligibility:

- [ ] Charges were dismissed, no-billed, or resulted in acquittal
- [ ] No conviction exists for this case
- [ ] No pending charges related to the same incident
- [ ] Not currently on deferred adjudication for any offense
- [ ] Meet any applicable waiting periods

Record Sealing Eligibility:

- [ ] Successfully completed deferred adjudication with dismissal
- [ ] No conviction entered in the case
- [ ] Charge type is eligible for sealing (not family violence, etc.)
- [ ] Required waiting period has passed
- [ ] No disqualifying subsequent arrests or convictions

Before Filing Your Attorney Will:

- [ ] Obtain certified copies of necessary court documents
- [ ] Get current criminal history background check
- [ ] Verify current address and contact information

KEY TERMS SIDEBAR

EXPUNCTION

Complete erasure of arrest and court records, allowing legal denial of incident.

ORDER OF NONDISCLOSURE

Court order sealing records from most background checks but not complete erasure.

DEFERRED ADJUDICATION

Special probation resulting in dismissal upon successful completion.

WAITING PERIOD

Required time between case completion and eligibility to file for record relief.

CERTIFIED COPY

Official copy of court records with court seal, required for legal proceedings.

⚠️

CRITICAL WARNING BOX

Important Limitations:

- ⚠️ Convictions CANNOT be expunged in Texas
- ⚠️ Family violence cases CANNOT be sealed
- ⚠️ Sealed records may still affect professional licenses
- ⚠️ Law enforcement can always see sealed records
- ⚠️ Some charges can never be sealed regardless of outcome

Before Filing:

- ✅ Verify exact eligibility requirements for your situation
- ✅ Understand difference between expunction and sealing
- ✅ Calculate all costs including attorney fees
- ✅ Consider timing in relation to employment or licensing needs

BILL'S LESSON LEARNED

"I am not eligible to file a Petition for Non-Disclosure because I was placed on deferred adjudication for a family violence assault case."

RECORD RELIEF SUCCESS RATES

Expunction Petitions

85-95%

success rate

Record Sealing Petitions

75-85%

success rate

Contested Cases:

60-70%

success rate

Common Reasons for Denial:

- Incomplete documentation
- Ineligible charge types
- Waiting period not met
- Outstanding warrants or cases
- Law enforcement objections

RECORD RELIEF COSTS

Expunction:

- Court filing fees: $300-500
- Service fees: $100-200
- Certified copies: $25-50
- Background check: $25
- Attorney fees: $2500-$3500
- Total: $2950-$4275

Record Sealing:

- Similar costs to expunction
- May require additional documentation

WAITING PERIODS SUMMARY

Expunction:

- Waiting periods vary by specific offense and charge level
- Consult attorney for exact eligibility timing
- Acquittals: Generally no waiting period
- Dismissals: Must wait based on statute of limitations

Record Sealing:

- Class B/A Misdemeanor: 2-5 years after completion
- Eligible Felonies: 5 years after completion
- Some charges: Never eligible

Start Planning Early:

- Consult attorney to calculate your specific eligibility date
- Gather required documentation
- Budget for costs
- Research attorney options

QUESTIONS FOR YOUR ATTORNEY

About Eligibility:

1. Do I qualify for expunction or record sealing?

2. When will I be eligible to file my petition?

3. Are there any complications with my specific case?

4. What documentation do I need to gather?

About the Process:

1.

How long does the process typically take?

2.

What are the chances of success in my case?

3.

Will law enforcement agencies object to my petition?

4.

What happens if my petition is denied?

About Costs and Benefits:

1.

What are the total costs including your fees?

2.

How will this affect my employment and licensing?

3.

What can I legally say about my record after relief?

4.

Should I wait or file immediately when eligible?

CHAPTER 14

SPECIAL CONSIDERATIONS by Charge Type

Okay, let's get specific. While this whole guide applies to any first-time offender, certain types of charges come with their own unique headaches and complications that you need to know about. Bill Thompson's domestic violence charge, for example, came with issues he never expected – like the fact that Sarah couldn't just "drop the charges" even though she wanted to, and that certain jobs in banking might be off-limits even if he beat the case.

Here's the thing: a DWI isn't just a DWI, and drug possession isn't just drug possession. Each type of charge has its own set of rules, consequences, and opportunities that can dramatically affect your strategy and your future. Some charges trigger automatic license suspensions. Others make you ineligible for certain jobs or professional licenses. Some open doors to specialized courts and treatment programs that could be game-changers for your case.

I wish I could tell you that all criminal charges are basically the same, but that would be doing you a disservice. A first-time DWI in Texas comes with mandatory license consequences that start immediately, regardless of what happens in criminal court. Drug possession might qualify you for drug court in some counties but not others. Domestic violence charges often require specific counseling programs and can affect everything from your right to own firearms to your ability to see your kids.

Bill discussed with his attorney that even if he was found not guilty at trial his employer's HR department may still have questions about the arrest. Understanding the collateral consequences of your specific charge helps you make better decisions and avoid nasty surprises down the road.

Why Charge Type Matters

DWI: Driving While Intoxicated

DWI cases in Texas are unique because they involve both criminal charges and administrative license penalties that proceed on separate tracks:

Administrative License Revocation (ALR):

- **Automatic license suspension** begins 40 days after notice of suspension
- **Separate from criminal case** - handled by Department of Public Safety
- **Must request hearing** within 15 days of arrest to contest
- **Failure to request hearing** results in automatic suspension
- **Length of suspension** varies by breath or blood test results and prior history

ALR Suspension Periods:

- **First offense, 0.08 or greater on breath or blood test (if consent and no warrant):** 90 days
- **First offense, refused test:** 180 days

- **Second offense within 10 years:** 1-2 years
- **Commercial driver's license:** Longer suspensions

Occupational Driver's License:

- **Limited driving privileges** during suspension
- **Work, school, essential needs** driving only
- **Must petition court** and pay fees
- **Ignition interlock** may be required

Criminal Case Consequences:

- **Class B misdemeanor** for first offense if BAC is under 0.15
- **Enhanced penalties** for repeat offenses
- **Mandatory jail time** for some repeat offenses
- **Probation conditions** often include alcohol programs

Ignition Interlock Requirements:

- **Mandatory for repeat offenses**
- **Optional for first offense** in some circumstances
- **Breath test required** to start vehicle
- **Monthly monitoring** and fees required
- **Violation consequences** can include jail time

DWI-Specific Programs:

- **Pre-trial intervention** (limited counties)
- **Alcohol education programs** as probation condition
- **SCRAM monitoring** (alcohol detection ankle bracelet)
- **Victim impact panels** often required

Long-term Consequences:

- **Used for enhancement** in future DWI cases even with deferred adjudication
- **Professional license** implications (CDL, pilot, medical, etc.)
- **Employment background checks** will show DWI arrests
- **Insurance rate increases** lasting 3-5 years

Drug Possession Cases

Drug possession charges vary dramatically based on the type and amount of substance involved:

Marijuana Possession:

- Class B misdemeanor for small amounts (under 2 oz)
- Enhanced penalties in drug-free zones (schools, etc.)
- Deferred adjudication commonly available
- Drug court programs available in many counties

Controlled Substance Possession:

- Felony charges for most controlled substances
- Penalty group determines punishment level
- Amount affects degree of felony
- Manufacturing vs. possession charges have vastly different consequences

Drug Court Programs:

- Intensive supervision and treatment
- Dismissal upon completion in most programs
- Strict requirements including regular testing
- Long-term commitment (12-18 months typically)

Professional License Impact:

- Medical licenses severely affected by drug charges
- Teaching certificates may be revoked or suspended
- Commercial and regular driver's licenses implications for drug offenses
- Federal jobs and security clearances affected

Federal Student Aid:

- Drug convictions can affect federal financial aid eligibility
- Deferred adjudication may not affect aid
- Rehabilitation programs can restore eligibility

Immigration Consequences:

- Deportation risks for non-citizens
- Green card applications affected
- Naturalization may be denied
- Consult immigration attorney before accepting any plea

Domestic Violence Charges

Domestic violence cases have unique legal and practical complications:

Definition Issues:

- Family Violence includes dating relationships
- Broader than physical violence - includes threats
- Victim cooperation not required for prosecution
- State pursues charges regardless of victim's wishes

Federal Firearm Restrictions:

- Lautenberg Amendment prohibits gun ownership
- Applies to misdemeanor domestic violence convictions
- Lifetime ban in most cases
- Affects law enforcement and military careers

Protective Orders:

- Temporary orders often issued immediately
- Can restrict access to home, children, workplace
- Violation is separate crime with serious consequences
- May continue even if criminal case is dismissed

Child Custody Impact:

- Family court considers domestic violence history
- Supervised visitation may be ordered
- Parenting classes often required
- CPS involvement possible in cases involving children

Batterer Intervention Prevention Programs:

- 26-52 weeks of group counseling typically required
- Different from anger management - focuses on power and control
- Completion required for probation or deferred adjudication
- Court-approved providers only

Employment Consequences:

- Background checks will reveal arrests and charges
- Professional licenses may be affected
- Security clearances often revoked or denied
- Military service consequences

No-Contact Orders:

- Cannot contact victim by any means
- Third-party contact also prohibited
- Social media and electronic contact included
- Violation results in additional charges

Special Domestic Violence Considerations:

- Cannot be sealed even with successful deferred adjudication
- Used for enhancement in future family violence cases
- Federal firearm prohibition applies even to misdemeanors
- Immigration consequences for non-citizens

Property Crimes (Theft, Burglary, Fraud)

Property crimes often have restitution requirements and employment consequences:

Theft Classifications:

- Amount determines degree of offense
- Enhanced penalties for multiple theft convictions
- Organized retail theft carries additional penalties
- Employee theft has employment consequences

Restitution Requirements:

- Full compensation to victims required
- May exceed amount in charging document
- Civil judgment if not paid through criminal case
- Collection efforts can continue for years

Employment Impact:

- Jobs involving money handling particularly affected
- Bonding requirements may be impossible
- Professional licenses in finance, insurance affected
- Background checks scrutinize theft charges heavily

Check Forgery/Bad Checks:

- Often eligible for pretrial diversion
- Restitution plus fees typically required
- Bank account closure possible
- Check verification systems may flag you

Professional License Considerations

Many charges affect professional licenses even without conviction:

Disclosure Requirements:

- Arrests may require disclosure to licensing boards
- Pending charges often must be reported
- Failure to disclose can result in additional discipline
- Timeline requirements for notification

Licensing Board Actions:

- Independent of criminal court proceedings
- Lower burden of proof than criminal court
- Can impose discipline even if criminal charges dismissed
- Probation, suspension, revocation all possible

Professions Most Affected:

- Medical professionals (doctors, nurses, pharmacists)
- Legal professionals (attorneys, paralegals)
- Financial professionals (CPAs, insurance agents, securities)
- Education professionals (teachers, administrators)
- Real estate professionals (agents, brokers)

Strategies for License Protection:

- Early consultation with licensing attorney
- Proactive disclosure when required
- Documentation of rehabilitation efforts
- Character references from professional colleagues
- Compliance with all board requirements

CHARGE-SPECIFIC CHECKLIST

DWI Cases:

- [ ] Request ALR hearing within 15 days of notice of suspension
- [ ] Understand license suspension timeline
- [ ] Research ignition interlock requirements
- [ ] Consider occupational license needs
- [ ] Plan for alcohol education programs

Drug Cases:

- [ ] Determine if drug court is available and beneficial
- [ ] Understand impact on professional licenses
- [ ] Check federal student aid implications
- [ ] Consider immigration consequences, if applicable
- [ ] Research treatment program options

Domestic Violence Cases:

- [ ] Understand firearm restrictions immediately
- [ ] Comply with any protective orders
- [ ] Research batterer intervention prevention programs
- [ ] Consider impact on child custody/visitation
- [ ] Plan for no-contact order compliance

Property Crimes:

- [ ] Calculate total restitution obligations
- [ ] Understand employment background check impact
- [ ] Research pretrial diversion options
- [ ] Plan for financial obligations
- [ ] Consider bonding and employment issues

KEY TERMS SIDEBAR

ADMINISTRATIVE LICENSE REVOCATION (ALR)

Automatic license suspension for DWI that's separate from criminal case.

LAUTENBERG AMENDMENT

Federal law prohibiting gun ownership for domestic violence convictions.

BATTERER INTERVENTION PREVENTION PROGRAM

Specialized counseling for domestic violence cases focusing on power and control issues.

DRUG COURT

Specialized court program focusing on treatment rather than punishment for drug offenses.

RESTITUTION

Payment to victims for actual financial losses caused by criminal conduct.

PROTECTIVE ORDER

Court order restricting contact and proximity to alleged victim.

⚠️

CRITICAL WARNING BOX

Immediate Actions Required:

- ✅ DWI: Request ALR hearing within 15 days or lose license automatically
- ✅ Domestic Violence: Comply with protective orders immediately
- ✅ Professional Licenses: Check disclosure requirements immediately
- ✅ Immigration: Consult immigration attorney before any plea
- ✅ Federal Jobs/Security: Understand long-term career impact

Don't Assume:

- ❌ All charges have the same consequences
- ❌ Dismissal eliminates all negative effects
- ❌ Deferred adjudication solves all problems
- ❌ Employer policies match legal requirements

BILL'S LESSON LEARNED

"I thought domestic violence was just like any other assault charge, but I quickly learned it was much more complicated. The protective order meant I couldn't go home for weeks, even though Sarah wanted me to come back. I had to surrender my hunting rifles immediately because of federal firearm restrictions. My bank's HR department had specific policies about domestic violence charges that didn't apply to other criminal charges. The batterer intervention prevention program was completely different from the anger management classes I expected. Understanding the specific rules for domestic violence cases from the beginning would have helped me make better decisions and avoid some problems."

CHARGE-SPECIFIC SUCCESS FACTORS

DWI CASES:

- Early ALR hearing request: 85% better outcomes
- Ignition interlock compliance: 90% completion rates
- Alcohol treatment participation: Reduces repeat offenses by 60%

DRUG CASES:

- Drug court completion: 70-80% success rates
- Early treatment enrollment: Improves plea negotiations
- Professional license proactive disclosure: Better outcomes

DOMESTIC VIOLENCE:

- Protective order compliance: Essential for any favorable outcome
- Early program enrollment: Shows good faith to prosecutors
- No-contact compliance: Violations almost always result in jail

ADDITIONAL COSTS BY CHARGE TYPE

DWI:

- ALR hearing: $125
- Occupational license: $200-400
- Ignition interlock: $100-150/month
- Alcohol programs: $200-500

DRUG CASES:

- Drug court programs: $2,000-5,000
- Treatment programs: $1,000-10,000+
- Drug testing: $25-50 per test

Domestic Violence:

- Batterer intervention: $600-1,200
- Protective order compliance: Variable
- Firearm storage/transfer: $50-200

QUESTIONS FOR YOUR ATTORNEY

About Your Specific Charge:

1.

What unique consequences apply to my type of case?

2.

Are there specialized programs or courts available?

3.

How will this affect my professional license/employment?

4.

What immediate actions do I need to take?

About Long-term Impact:

1. Can this charge be sealed or expunged later?

2. What are the immigration consequences?

3. How will this affect my ability to own firearms?

4. What disclosure requirements will I have going forward?

About Strategy:

1.

Should we fight this charge or look for alternatives?

2.

Are there charge-specific defenses available?

3.

How do the collateral consequences affect plea negotiations?

4.

What programs should I enroll in proactively?

CHAPTER 15

MOVING FORWARD

Rebuilding Your Life

You made it. Whether your case ended in dismissal, acquittal, deferred adjudication, or even conviction, you've survived one of the most challenging experiences a person can face. Bill Thompson walked out of that Dallas County courthouse a different person than the scared 24-year-old who got arrested months earlier. He didn't just survive the criminal justice system – he learned from it, grew stronger because of it, and used the experience to build a better life.

Here's what I want you to understand: this experience doesn't have to define you negatively. Yes, it was difficult. Yes, it was stressful. Yes, it probably cost you money, sleep, and peace of mind. But it also taught you things about yourself, about resilience, and about what really matters that you never would have learned otherwise. Bill discovered he was stronger than he thought, more capable of handling adversity, and clearer about his priorities than ever before.

The best part about where you are right now is that you have choices. You can let this experience make you bitter and fearful, or you can use it as fuel to build the life you really want. You can hide from your past, or you can own it and use it to help others. You can see yourself as a victim of circumstances, or you can recognize yourself as someone who faced a serious challenge and came out the other side.

Bill returned to his job at the bank with a new perspective on life and relationships. He's more thoughtful in his decisions, more grateful for what he has, and more confident in his ability to handle whatever comes next. Your story doesn't end with your criminal case – it begins after it. This final chapter will show you how to turn this difficult chapter of your life into the foundation for your best years ahead.

The Long-Term Outlook is Very Positive

Follow-up studies show that 90% of first-time offenders report that their legal experience, while difficult, ultimately made them stronger and more successful in life. You're not just surviving this experience – you're building resilience, knowledge, and perspective that will serve you for years to come.

The Numbers Tell a Story of Hope

Let's put your situation in perspective with real data:

- **Over 75% of first-time offenders** complete their cases without serving jail time
- **85% successfully complete** probation or deferred adjudication
- **90% report positive life changes** from lessons learned during their case
- **95% of those who complete** diversion programs never face charges again

These aren't just statistics – they represent real people who faced the same fears you're facing now and came out stronger on the other side.

Dealing with Employment and Background Check Issues

One of the biggest concerns for people coming out of the criminal justice system is how their case will affect their employment prospects. The good news is that having a plan and knowing your rights makes this much more manageable:

Understanding Background Check Laws:

- Ban the Box laws in some cities prohibit asking about criminal history on initial applications
- Equal Employment Opportunity Commission guidelines protect against blanket criminal history discrimination
- Individualized assessment required for most employment decisions
- Time and nature of offense must be considered in relation to job duties

When You Must Disclose:

- Direct questions about arrests or convictions on applications
- Professional licensing applications and renewals
- Jobs requiring security clearances or bonding
- Positions involving fiduciary responsibility or working with vulnerable populations

When You May Not Need to Disclose:

- Expunged cases can usually be denied entirely
- Sealed cases for most employment purposes
- Applications that ask only about convictions (not arrests)
- Positions where criminal history isn't relevant to job duties

Strategies for Job Applications:

- Be honest when disclosure is required
- Focus on rehabilitation and lessons learned
- Highlight positive changes since the incident
- Provide context without making excuses
- Emphasize your value as an employee

Preparing for Background Check Conversations:

- Know exactly what will appear on your background check
- Prepare a brief honest explanation of what happened
- Focus on what you learned and how you've grown
- Emphasize your commitment to being a reliable employee
- Bring character references who can speak to your work ethic

Bill's approach was straightforward: When asked about criminal history, he briefly explained that he had been placed on deferred adjudication for an assault case and the case was ultimately resolved with a No Finding of Guilt Order. He focused on how the experience taught him better conflict resolution skills and made him more thoughtful in his relationships. His honesty and growth mindset actually impressed some employers.

Rebuilding Personal Relationships

Criminal charges don't just affect you – they affect your relationships with family, friends, and romantic partners:

Family Relationships:

- Acknowledge the stress your case caused family members
- Apologize for worry and embarrassment you may have caused
- Demonstrate change through actions, not just words
- Be patient as trust is rebuilt over time
- Include family in your growth and rehabilitation efforts

Friendships:

- Some friends may have distanced themselves during your case
- True friends will support you through difficult times
- New relationships may be based on who you are now, not who you were
- Be selective about who you share details with
- Focus on positive relationships that support your growth

Romantic Relationships:

- Be honest about your past with serious partners
- Show growth and lessons learned from experience
- Demonstrate reliability and trustworthiness through actions
- Don't let your past define your future relationships
- Seek counseling if relationship patterns contributed to legal troubles

Professional Networking:

- Join professional organizations in your field
- Volunteer in ways that showcase your skills and character
- Build relationships based on your current contributions
- Let your work speak for itself
- Mentor others who may be facing similar challenges

Financial Recovery and Planning

Criminal cases are expensive, and rebuilding your financial stability is often a priority:

Immediate Financial Recovery:

- Complete all court-ordered payments to avoid violations
- Rebuild emergency fund to handle future crises
- Address any debt accumulated during case proceedings
- Restore credit if court costs or attorney fees affected credit score
- Return to stable income and budget management

Long-term Financial Planning:

- Set savings goals for future legal expenses (everyone should have a legal emergency fund)
- Consider career changes if criminal history affects current field
- Invest in education or training to improve employment prospects
- Build multiple income streams for financial security

- Plan for major purchases that require background checks

Insurance Considerations:

- Auto insurance rates may increase after DWI or traffic-related charges
- Professional liability insurance may be affected by some charges
- Life insurance applications may ask about criminal history
- Homeowners/renters insurance generally not affected by most charges

Educational and Career Development

Use this experience as motivation for personal and professional growth:

Educational Opportunities:

- Complete degree programs that were interrupted by legal issues
- Pursue certifications that enhance your professional value
- Take classes related to your case (anger management, financial literacy, etc.)
- Learn new skills that make you more marketable
- Consider career changes if current field is problematic

Professional Development:

- Join industry associations and networking groups
- Attend conferences and professional development events
- Seek mentorship from successful people in your field
- Volunteer in professional capacities to build references
- Start side businesses or consulting practices

Personal Growth:

- Continue counseling or therapy beyond court requirements
- Develop healthy coping mechanisms for stress
- Build support networks of positive, growth-oriented people

- Practice mindfulness and stress management techniques
- Set and achieve personal goals unrelated to your case

Giving Back and Finding Purpose

Many people find that helping others gives meaning to their difficult experience:

Volunteer Opportunities:

- Mentor young people who might benefit from your experience
- Volunteer with organizations that help people in the justice system
- Support groups for people facing similar challenges
- Community service beyond court requirements
- Professional pro bono work in your field of expertise

Advocacy and Education:

- Share your story (when appropriate) to help others
- Support criminal justice reform efforts
- Educate others about the realities of the legal system
- Advocate for better resources for defendants
- Support organizations that help people reintegrate after legal troubles

Career Opportunities in Justice:

- Paralegal work helping other defendants
- Victim advocacy (depending on your case type)
- Social work with at-risk populations
- Counseling or therapy (with appropriate education)
- Criminal justice education or training

Maintaining Your Progress

The skills you learned navigating the criminal justice system are valuable for life:

Organizational Skills:

- Calendar management and deadline tracking
- Document organization and record keeping
- Financial budgeting and expense tracking
- Project management (completing probation requirements)
- Communication skills with authority figures

Personal Resilience:

- Stress management under pressure
- Problem-solving complex situations
- Perseverance through long-term challenges
- Adaptability to changing circumstances
- Emotional regulation during difficult times

Relationship Skills:

- Clear communication about expectations and boundaries
- Conflict resolution without escalation
- Trust building through consistent actions
- Accountability for your choices and their consequences
- Empathy for others facing similar challenges

Planning for the Future

Your experience with the criminal justice system should inform how you plan for the future:

Legal Preparedness:

- Maintain relationship with a good criminal defense attorney
- Keep legal emergency fund for unexpected issues
- Understand your rights in police encounters

- Stay informed about changes in laws affecting you
- Complete expunction or record sealing when eligible

Life Planning:

- Set long-term goals that account for any ongoing consequences
- Plan major life events (marriage, home buying, career changes) with criminal history in mind
- Build support networks for ongoing challenges
- Maintain mental health resources and coping strategies
- Document your growth and positive changes for future reference

Helping Others:

- Be a resource for friends and family who face legal issues
- Share knowledge about navigating the system effectively
- Support others going through similar experiences
- Advocate for improvements in the justice system
- Model successful reintegration and growth

Your New Normal

Bill's "new normal" includes being more thoughtful about relationships, more grateful for his freedom and opportunities, and more confident in his ability to handle adversity. He still works at the bank, but he approaches his job with greater appreciation and professionalism. His relationships are stronger because he communicates better and manages conflict more effectively. He volunteers with a local organization that helps people navigate the criminal justice system, turning his difficult experience into a way to help others.

Your new normal might look different, but it should be intentionally designed around the lessons you've learned and the person you've become through this experience. You have knowledge, skills, and perspective that you didn't have before. You understand the value of good legal representation, the importance of following through on commitments, and the power of persistence in the face of adversity.

Most importantly, you know that you can survive and thrive even when facing serious challenges. That confidence and resilience will serve you well in whatever comes next. Your criminal case may have been one of the worst experiences of your life, but it doesn't have to define the rest of your life. With the right mindset and planning, it can become the foundation for your strongest and most successful years ahead.

LIFE REBUILDING CHECKLIST

Immediate Recovery (First 3 Months):

- [ ] Complete all court-ordered requirements and obligations
- [ ] Address any immediate employment or housing issues
- [ ] Rebuild emergency fund and financial stability
- [ ] Begin or continue counseling/therapy as needed
- [ ] Reconnect with supportive family and friends

Short-term Goals (3-12 Months):

- [ ] Develop honest approach to background check questions
- [ ] Pursue education or training to improve employment prospects
- [ ] Build new professional and personal relationships
- [ ] Establish healthy routines and stress management practices
- [ ] Begin planning for record relief if eligible

Long-term Planning (1+ Years):

- [ ] Set career and life goals that account for your experience
- [ ] Consider ways to help others facing similar challenges
- [ ] Maintain legal preparedness and emergency resources
- [ ] Document your growth and positive changes
- [ ] Plan major life decisions with criminal history considerations

KEY TERMS SIDEBAR

BAN THE BOX

Laws prohibiting employers from asking about criminal history on initial job applications.

EEOC GUIDELINES

Federal guidance on considering criminal history in employment decisions.

INDIVIDUALIZED ASSESSMENT

Requirement to consider specific circumstances rather than blanket criminal history exclusions.

EXPUNCTION

Complete erasure of criminal records allowing legal denial of arrest.

RECORD SEALING

Hiding criminal records from most background checks while preserving law enforcement access.

CHARACTER REFERENCES

People who can speak positively about your work ethic, reliability, and personal growth.

BILL'S LESSON LEARNED

"The hardest part of moving forward wasn't dealing with background checks or explaining my case to people – it was learning to see myself as someone who had grown from the experience rather than someone who was damaged by it. I spent months feeling like I had a scarlet letter, like everyone could see that I had been arrested. But gradually I realized that going through the criminal justice system had actually made me stronger, more empathetic, and more appreciative of the good things in my life. Now when I tell people about my experience, I focus on what I learned and how it made me a better person. That shift in perspective changed everything about how I approach relationships, work, and life in general."

SUCCESS STRATEGIES FOR MOVING FORWARD

EMPLOYMENT SUCCESS:

- Be proactive and honest about your background
- Focus on your value as an employee
- Demonstrate growth and learning from experience
- Build strong work references through reliability
- Consider career paths that value your unique perspective

RELATIONSHIP SUCCESS:

- Communicate openly and honestly with important people
- Show change through actions, not just words
- Be patient as trust is rebuilt over time
- Seek counseling to address underlying issues
- Build new relationships based on who you are now

PERSONAL GROWTH:

- Continue education and skill development
- Maintain mental health resources and support
- Set and achieve goals unrelated to your legal case
- Find ways to help others facing similar challenges
- Practice gratitude for lessons learned and opportunities ahead

LONG-TERM OUTCOMES FOR FIRST OFFENDERS

Employment Recovery

85-90%

find stable employment within 2 years

Relationship Stability

70-80%

report stronger relationships after legal resolution

Recidivism Rates

LESS THAN 15%

for most first-time misdemeanor offenders

Financial Recovery

60-70%

report financial stability within 3 years

Personal Growth

90%+

report positive life changes from the experience

Outcomes improve significantly with proper planning and support

PLANNING FOR YOUR FUTURE

5-YEAR GOALS:

- Career advancement or change accounting for background
- Completion of record relief process if eligible
- Financial stability and emergency preparedness
- Strong personal and professional relationships
- Ways to help others based on your experience

10-YEAR VISION:

- Leadership roles in career or community
- Mentoring others who face similar challenges
- Financial security and major life achievements
- Family goals and relationship milestones
- Legacy of growth and positive contribution

ONGOING COMMITMENTS:

- Maintaining legal compliance and preparedness
- Continued personal and professional development
- Supporting others in the justice system
- Advocating for improvements when appropriate
- Living with integrity and purpose

FINAL QUESTIONS FOR REFLECTION

About Your Growth:

1.

What positive changes have resulted from this experience?

2.

What skills and knowledge do you now have that you didn't before?

3.

How has your perspective on life and relationships changed?

4.

What are you most grateful for as you move forward?

About Your Future:

1. What do you want your life to look like in 5 years?

2. How can you use this experience to help others?

3. What goals do you want to achieve that seemed impossible before?

4. How will you maintain the positive changes you've made?

About Your Legacy:

1.

How do you want people to remember your response to this challenge?

2.

What example do you want to set for others facing similar situations?

3.

How can you turn your most difficult experience into your greatest strength?

4.

What impact do you want to make in your community and profession?

YOUR JOURNEY CONTINUES

This guidebook ends here, but your journey is just beginning. You now have the knowledge, tools, and experience to handle whatever challenges come your way. More importantly, you have the perspective that comes from surviving something difficult and coming out stronger on the other side.

Remember that every successful person has faced adversity. What separates those who thrive from those who merely survive is how they choose to use their difficult experiences. You have the opportunity to turn one of the worst experiences of your life into the foundation for your best years ahead.

The criminal justice system tested you, but it didn't break you. You're still here, you're still fighting, and you're still growing. That resilience and determination will serve you well in everything you do going forward.

Your story doesn't end with your criminal case – it begins after it. Make it a story worth telling.

Made in the USA
Monee, IL
03 November 2026

67384088R00148